HALFWAY BITCHES GO STRAIGHT TO HEAVEN

HALFWAY BITCHES GO STRAIGHT TO HEAVEN

Stephen Adly Guirgis

THEATRE COMMUNICATIONS GROUP / NEW YORK / 2022

Halfway Bitches Go Straight to Heaven is published by Theatre Communications Group, Inc., 520 Eighth Avenue, 24th Floor, New York, NY 10018-4156

Excerpt, page 99: Hughes, Langston. *The Weary Blues*. New York: Alfred A. Knopf, 1926.

The publication of *Halfway Bitches Go Straight to Heaven* by Stephen Adly Guirgis, through TCG Books, is made possible with support by Mellon Foundation.

Special thanks to Betsy Pitts for her generous support of this publication.

TCG books are exclusively distributed to the book trade by Consortium Book Sales and Distribution.

Library of Congress Control Numbers:
2021051587 (print) / 2021051588 (ebook)
ISBN 978-1-55936-989-3 (paperback) / ISBN 978-1-55936-942-8 (ebook)
A catalog record for this book is available from the Library of Congress.

Book design and composition by Lisa Govan
Cover design by Joan Wong

First Edition, November 2022
Second Printing, March 2023

PREFACE

Back in the day, when I was a young acting student and a full-time fuckup, a well-known actor came to our class to talk about how to "make it in the business." I was terrible at the business of the business (I still am) and I was terrible mainly because I was absolutely fucking terrified (I mostly still am) and I lacked confidence in myself, my appearance, and my abilities (mostly still do). I remember being very impressed and inspired by the speaker that day, taking notes and hanging on his every word. He had the magic formula. And I wanted that shit. We all did. And then, right around the part where they tell you how hard it is, how shitty it is, how you have to be willing to starve, how unlikely it is you'll ever earn a living, and if there's anything else you can do besides acting you should go do that instead (none of that shit fazed me), he suddenly looked straight at me and said: "For all these reasons—and trust me on this because I've seen it a million times—if you do not have 100% faith and belief in yourself that you can do this, if you don't KNOW it— then please quit now because I promise no one will believe in you and you will go nowhere and you will waste your life." And

PRODUCTION HISTORY

Halfway Bitches Go Straight to Heaven had its world premiere at Atlantic Theater Company (Neil Pepe, Artistic Director; Jeffory Lawson, Managing Director), in partnership with LAByrinth Theater Company (John Ortiz, Artistic Director), in New York City on November 15, 2019. It was directed by John Ortiz. The scenic design was by Narelle Sissons, the lighting design was by Mary Louise Geiger, the costume design was by Alexis Forte, the sound design and original music were by Elisheba Ittoop; the production stage manager was Chris De Camillis. The cast was:

SARGE	Liza Colón-Zayas
MUNCHIES	Pernell Walker
LITTLE MELBA DIAZ	Kara Young
ROCKAWAY ROSIE	Elizabeth Canavan
BETTY WOODS	Kristina Poe
WANDA WHEELS	Patrice Johnson Chevannes
TAINA	Viviana Valeria
HAPPY MEAL SONIA	Wilemina Olivia-Garcia
QUEEN SUGAR	Benja Kay Thomas
BELLA/CHIEF OF STAFF AMY GOLDEN	Andrea Syglowski
VENUS RAMIREZ	Esteban Andres Cruz
MATEO	Sean Carvajal
MISS RIVERA	Elizabeth Rodriguez

CHARACTERS

SARGE: Female decorated war vet. PTSD. Bipolar. Violent.

MUNCHIES: Single mother. Under the spell of Sarge.

LITTLE MELBA DIAZ: Teenage poet. Survivor. Admirer of Sarge.

ROCKAWAY ROSIE: Alcoholic. Miss Lonely Heart.

BETTY WOODS: A shut-in turned homeless self-published author.

WANDA WHEELS: Once a cultured artist and a drunk. Still is.

TAINA: She won't leave her damaged mother.

HAPPY MEAL SONIA: Taina's mother. Can't function in society.

QUEEN SUGAR: An ex-con hungry for opportunity.

BELLA: Sarge's girl. Stripper, recovering addict, with a baby.

VENUS RAMIREZ: Trans. Salty of tongue/honey of heart.

MATEO: Seventeen-year-old son of a terminally ill resident.

MISS RIVERA: Overworked, tough and unbowed. She runs the place.

FATHER MIGUEL: Radical Jesuit. Second-in-command. Mentors Mateo.

JENNIFER: Young well-meaning white social worker.

MR. MOBO: A social worker originally from Nigeria.

JOEY FRESCO: Born-again ex-con. Janitor. In love with Venus.

NICKY: He beat up his wife. His dad did worse to him.

DETECTIVE SULLIVAN: Bullshit depresses him.

CHIEF OF STAFF AMY GOLDEN: Ambitious politician's aide.

PLACE

The action of the play takes place in and around Hope House: a government-funded residence for women, providing transitional shelter and support for women in need in New York City.

Act One

SCENE 1

Talent Night in the Community Room.

In blackout, Bach's Cello Suite no. 1 is being performed with great feeling. It ends with a flourish—and is met by dead silence.

Lights up. In the room is Mateo, Sugar, Munchies, Melba, Sonia, Taina, Rosie, Venus, Joey, Wanda, Bella and Sarge.

A man in a dashiki and slacks, Mobo, claps loudly.

MR. MOBO: Ah! Wonderful! Sheer delight! Ladies, please!! A nice hand for our guest from the conservatory—Stacy Wu— Where's Miss Wu? Miss Wu, come back—Miss Wu? Miss Wu?

MATEO: Yo Mister Mobo—that Miss Wu bitch was wack!

MR. MOBO: Mateo!

MATEO: My bad, Mister Mobo. But wack is wack!

(Mobo whips out a tiny notepad, writing as he speaks—)

MR. MOBO: "Wack is wack," I see.

MATEO: You see what?—

MR. MOBO: I see your name on my report—now YOU are wack! . . .

MATEO: Aw, c'mon, Mister Mobo!

MR. MOBO: Ladies! Some announcements before our next contestant: *(Reading quickly)* Incest survivors meeting has moved to the basement. Memorial service for our Keisha Thomas to be held Thursday at Mott Haven Academy in the Bronx—

QUEEN SUGAR: Keisha ain't dead!!

MUNCHIES: You thinking of Ta'Nisha.

QUEEN SUGAR: I know the difference 'tween Keisha and Ta'Nisha!!!

MUNCHIES: So do I: That hi-yella thievin' bitch Ta'Nisha still breathin'—Little Keisha dead!

MR. MOBO: Sunday workshop: "You, Me and Hepatitis C" now includes pancake breakfast.

QUEEN SUGAR: Hold up! What?! You mean Little Keisha?! The little one?! *(To Melba)* Melba—your friend Keisha?

LITTLE MELBA DIAZ: Yeah.

QUEEN SUGAR: Oh I'm sorry, baby!

MR. MOBO: Loitering is not permitted outside the building—

QUEEN SUGAR: Mobo! Be more specific next time! You said "Keisha" not "Little Keisha"!

MR. MOBO: But there's only one Keisha.

QUEEN SUGAR: But we know her as Little Keisha!

MR. MOBO: So where is Big Keisha then?! Locate me Big Keisha!

QUEEN SUGAR: Locate you?! *(To Munchies)* What the fuck he talkin' about?

MUNCHIES: I don't know, but he pretty—and he packing thunder in them slacks.

HAPPY MEAL SONIA: I want pizza!!!!!!

MUNCHIES *(To Sugar)*: I'm a fuck that nigga—watch!

MR. MOBO: Section 8 Housing!

HAPPY MEAL SONIA: Pizza!!!

MR. MOBO: Section 8 choice voucher applications are available only through HUD at 26 Federal Plaza—Miss Soto does not have them so don't ask.

HAPPY MEAL SONIA: Pizza!

MR. MOBO: Pizza is served after the talent show.

HAPPY MEAL SONIA: What'd he say?

TAINA: He said no pizza now—

HAPPY MEAL SONIA: No pizza??!! But I want pizza! They said pizza!

TAINA: Pizza later, Ma—

(Sonia starts to cry like a wounded child.)

HAPPY MEAL SONIA: They said pizza! They said pizza!

ROCKAWAY ROSIE: Oh for cryin' out loud—can't we just go to bed now?!

TAINA: Mister Mobo!! How 'bout a little slice for my moms, please?!

MR. MOBO: Taina, your mother must refrain—

TAINA: Refrain??! Refrain how??!! Pizza will fuckin' refrain her—

HAPPY MEAL SONIA: They said pizza! They said—penis! Penis??! Oh no! Penis penis!!

TAINA: No, penis, Ma, no penis . . . Mobo, please—my mom needs pizza!

HAPPY MEAL SONIA: Penis! Uh-oh—penis! Penis!

ROCKAWAY ROSIE: Oh Christ—here we go again!

HAPPY MEAL SONIA: Penis penis! Diablo penis! No mas penis penis! Oh no!

QUEEN SUGAR: Give her the pizza so she can shut the fuck up!!

WANDA WHEELS: Give it up, Mobo—you're not guarding the gold mines of Bin Yauri, it's just damn PIZZA!

HAPPY MEAL SONIA: Penis penis! I can't breathe! I can't—Ay! Taina— ¡El pinga malvado me está asfixiando! ¡Ayúdeme! ¡Ayúdeme! Penis penis! ¡Pinga pinga!

VENUS RAMIREZ: Ay! Cajate with the "Pinga pinga"! Mister Mobo! Put on *Real Housewives* already! And put this La Loca Happy Meal Sonia back to Bellevue where she belongs! ¡Pa fuera!

TAINA: Yo shut your gay homo faggot ass, Venus! I'll beat the bitch off you! Niggas with dicks ain't even supposed to be here!

VENUS RAMIREZ: Oh look who's squawking! Twenny something and still sucking on mami's tetas! Yo Mobo—don't call Bellevue, call Ringling Brothers—put these two circus bitches in the clown car sweeping elephant poo—

HAPPY MEAL SONIA: Poo??!! Poo—penis!!! Penis penis!!

MR. MOBO: Mister Fresco—please!

HAPPY MEAL SONIA: Poo poo penis! No mas pinga penis—no mas—ay!

(Joey subdues and escorts Sonia and Taina.)

JOEY FRESCO: Calmate, mami.

TAINA: She just needed pizza! She got blood sugar, okay?!

(Taina turns to Venus—)

And you! You're fuckin' DEAD, puta!! Ask around—I don't fuckin' play!

VENUS RAMIREZ: Ay por favor—

TAINA: ¡¡"Por favor" nada, coño tu madre!!—I got mad peoples, yo! Affiliated motherfuckers who'll dead a faggot nigga like you just to pass time! Yeah—they gonna stab you up, make faggot burgers out your ass!! Gonna have a Venus Ramirez barbecue on Orchard Beach—serve you up on

Salsa Sunday with arroz con gondules, ya puta ho—dick-having bitch!

(Sonia is singing and laughing now, as they exit:)

HAPPY MEAL SONIA: "Dick-having bitch, dick-having bitch"—

(Sonia slips out of Joey's hold, and starts busting Michael Jackson moves.)

Dick have-er, duck hunter—oh!!

(Sonia falls over. Taina and Joey help her out the door. Pause.)

MR. MOBO: . . . Well. So I think, perhaps, no more talent show . . . I think everyone go to bed—

(Sarge rises from her seat.)

SARGE: But yo, Mobo: the kid—she ain't performed yet.
LITTLE MELBA DIAZ: Nah, nah, it's okay, Mister Mobo, I don't have to—
SARGE: C'mon, Mobo, you got her little card right there in your hands—
LITTLE MELBA DIAZ: Nah, Mister Mobo—I don't wanna.
WANDA WHEELS: Melba?
LITTLE MELBA DIAZ: Yes, Miss Wanda?
WANDA WHEELS: I had a thought. Would it help if maybe Mister Mobo turned off all the lights so you could feel alone and private—
MR. MOBO: This is not a good idea!
ROCKAWAY ROSIE: Come on, Mobo, live a little.
SARGE: Mateo—hit the lights.

(Mateo goes to the light switch.)

MATEO: Mister Mobo—can I?

MR. MOBO: Melba, you are a good girl. Not like these older ladies here who live to make trouble for me.

ROCKAWAY ROSIE: . . . Oh Mobo—dry up!

(The women giggle.)

MR. MOBO: Laugh, yes. Big humor! But I'm the one who'll catch the devil from Miss Rivera, so— Number one, if I turn off the lights, you must all "chill on it."

(Giggles.)

BELLA *(To Sarge)*: Did he say "chill on it"?—

MR. MOBO: Number two: Pick up the cigarette butts from outside the building and tidy your sleeping area before Miss Rivera arrives in the morning. Number three—

SARGE: Three?!

QUEEN SUGAR: Mobo getting greedy now.

MR. MOBO: Number three—*Venus*—you will squash your dispute with Taina and her mother and you will apologize before it escalates—

(Sarge stands and applauds.)

SARGE: Dass right, Mobo!!! *(To Venus)* And then—transfer your ugly, non-passing fake she-male junkie ass to a MEN'S residence cuz you a goddamn man!

MUNCHIES: And a greazy, skank-ass, fug-lified motherfuckah to boot!

(They nod and high five.)

VENUS RAMIREZ: Jealous hags—look who's talking! I'm fine as fuck with the mens lined up—meanwhile, you two Jurassic Park–looking bitches—y'all be waddling down the street and peoples be like: "Oh snap! Yabba Dabba Doo Times Two!" Fuckin' "Meet the Negrita Flintstones" an' shit!

MR. MOBO: Ladies, ladies—   BELLA *(To Sarge)*: Let it go.

SARGE: Don't be calling Venus no lady, Mister Mobo—look at him! Not only is he a fuckin' dude with a five-dollar perm—but he look like a minimum-wage Mexican midget dishwasher whose Moms got gang-banged by a pack of gap-toothed, Jheri-curled chupacabras an' shit!

BELLA: Really?—

MUNCHIES: "Chupacabras"! You nailed that nigga, girl!

(Venus is stung by this attack. She stares daggers at Sarge.)

SARGE: Truth hurts, don't it, faggot? Wha? You wanna do something about it?

BELLA: Stop it—

VENUS RAMIREZ: I have every right to be here.

MR. MOBO: Sarge, she has the right!

SARGE: This a residence for WOMEN, Mobo.

VENUS RAMIREZ: I am a woman, and I ain't going anywhere.

SARGE: You a selfish cocksucker is what you are. I know your type: can't make it in a men's shelter cuz they'll rape your ass, so you take advantage of some bullshit PC government loophole and fuck over all the REAL FEMALE VICTIMS desperate for a safe fuckin' space!

QUEEN SUGAR: Sarge ain't wrong!

MUNCHIES: Nigga need to go!

MR. MOBO: Munchies, Sugar, Sarge—

SARGE: C'mon, Mobo! You KNOW there ain't but so many beds for women in this city—and right now, this tranny bitch's junkie man-dick is taking a real woman's bed—and costing a REAL-LIFE woman her REAL-LIFE life!

VENUS RAMIREZ: I am a real-life woman!

SARGE: You ain't no woman!

MR. MOBO: Sarge!

BELLA: I know what you're doing—knock it off—

SARGE: Nah fuck that! You wanna be a woman? Chop off yo dick! Need help? I'll do that shit for you, Benihana-style! Cuz right now—tonight—there's a woman in fuckin' danger out there somewhere and she can't come here BECAUSE OF YOU!

VENUS RAMIREZ: I respectfully disagree.

SARGE: You don't "*respect-fully*" shit! Like before! That crazy Happy Meal Sonia just had her twice-a-day insane mental conniption—you think that wack-a-doo bitch's loud-ass penis penis shit don't bother the fuck out of all of us?!

QUEEN SUGAR: Preach sister!!

ROCKAWAY ROSIE: Oh, oh—Amen, yes!

SARGE: But we don't fuck with her, and I don't do shit, and no one says shit—cuz we got courtesy, okay—plus—bitch got a daughter! But you?! You ain't even supposed to be here and you act like this the Ramada Inn and everything supposed to be all nice. Well it ain't. And neither the fuck are you!

MR. MOBO: Sarge!

SARGE: Hold up. One more thing.

(Sarge calls out Betty who sits in the very back corner.)

You! Fat bitch in the corner! Yeah you! Our "collective courtesy" here?! It extend to Crazy Bitches—but the warranty runs out quick on Stinky Bitches! So take a fuckin' shower, Fatty MacWhitey—and consider yourself warned!!!

BELLA *(To Betty)*: She doesn't mean that—
SARGE: Oh yes I do!
QUEEN SUGAR: Sarge for President, yo!!!

(Venus rises angrily, crosses to Sarge—)

VENUS RAMIREZ: You're ignorant, Sarge! And a bully! And you're fuckin' wrong!

(Sarge quickly gets in Venus's face.)

SARGE: And you a Nancy Boy, pig-wigged faggot! Whatchu wanna do?!
BELLA: Carmen!
MR. MOBO: No fighting!
VENUS RAMIREZ: I'm gonna pray for you. Three Novenas to Nuestra Señora de Altagracia on your behalf.
SARGE: Pray for yourself, mister. Because if you don't go upstairs, pack up your shit, and take your ugly man-dick ass the fuck out of where it don't belong—it's gonna get realer than real up in here!
VENUS RAMIREZ: Ya know what? I've had a long day. I'm going to go upstairs, paint my toenails, eat a Snickers bar—curl up with my trashy romance novella from the library and gently fall to blissful slumber. Fact: your hatred—that's your problem. Because my right to be here is federally protected under Title IX of the 1972 Education Amendment to the United States Constitution. I'm here. I'm federal. Get used to it. And if you gotta problem with that—don't blame me—blame an immensely missed fine-ass motherfucker by the name of Barack Hussein Obama!

(Venus does a dramatic turn and begins exiting. Sarge calls out to her:)

SARGE: Obama?! Nah, nigga! Obama ain't trying to sleep here—
you are!! And Obama's my people—he ain't none of yours!

(Bella rises from her seat next to Sarge, goes to exit.)

Where you going?
BELLA: I just can't with you right now . . . Venus!

(Bella exits.)

SARGE: Can't with *me*?! That motherfucker just tried to claim
Obama! I got a photo with Obama—do he??!! No!!! . . .
C'mon, Bella—you seen the fuckin' photo! Bella!
    (To the group) Okay, I know y'all seen the photo! . . .
    (Referring to Bella) Shit—bitch walk out on me?! That's
"white privilege" right there. Bitch got the burger, think
she got the right to the bun! Fuck that. Gonna straighten
that out right quick. Her—and that "Title 9 No Titty"
bitch. "Federal"?! Federal my ass!!!

*(A beat. Sarge starts to cry a little. Munchies hands her a
Kleenex.)*

MUNCHIES: Here.

(Sarge dabs.)

MR. MOBO: Sarge—Little Melba has been waiting patiently. Are
you through now?
SARGE: Yeah. My apologies.
MR. MOBO: Do I need to put you on report for making threats?
SARGE: Nah, Mobo, nah. But still: fuck you too.
MR. MOBO: "F— me," sure. I cut you slack, you cut me,
"F— me." I don't know. Maybe submit your DNA to

Ancestry dot com. Perhaps Bella learned white privilege from you . . . Okay then. Mateo: lights, please.

(Mateo turns out the lights. The stage goes black. Mobo lights a lighter, reads from a card:)

. . . So, yes, our final participant, she's from the third floor, she's in ninth grade, and she enjoys "poetry, dank blueberry kush and Cardi B." I don't know. But here she is, Little Melba Diaz.

(Mobo passes Melba the lighter. She alone is lit. She is very shy. Nervous. She opens her notebook, clears her throat, holds the lighter and reads tentatively:)

LITTLE MELBA DIAZ: Hi. Okay . . .

Halfway bitches go straight to Heaven
I ex-caped foster care and met a boy named Kevin
He was the apple of my eye but nigga turned into a lemon
So I quit his narrow ass and got with his cousin Devin
Dev was fly but always high, plus the violence and bad
    breath,
So I went with his uncle, but his ass got shot to death,
Tio hadn't paid the rent, so we all got evicted,
I moved in with a dealer but he got raided and convicted
I was pregnant and homeless, I had no place to go,
No money in my pocket, I was feeling kinda low,
I met a pimp named Jacuzzi, he turnt me out to be his ho,
But then my belly got too big and business got too slow
So he gave me to an Uber driver, who at first was very kind
Then he started doing shit to me that'd blow your fuckin'
    mind
I prayed that God would save me and protect my unborn
    seed

Guess the good Lord gone fishin' in my greatest hour of
   need
After I lost my baby—well—
Words are turds and rhymes are crimes
Memories mere summaries,
Though I might someday share some of these
But the upshot: and I'll spare you the overwrought what-not,
Mister Uber fell asleep at a truck stop, I hit the jackpot,
   took a snapshot, ran off like a motherfucking gunshot,
   then came back to hang like a boomerang—cuz as an
   afterthought,
I left him with an onslaught of a forget-me-not
A brick did the trick, some dude pulled me off him
Before I put him in his coffin
I hopped the Amtrak to Penn Station planning to die by
   rope or razor—
But on that train was Father Miguel
Who became my friend-savior
Now I live here with y'all, in Room 307
Halfway bitches got it hard—
But we going straight to Heaven.

The end.

(She blows out the flame. Blackout.)

SCENE 2

Building Exterior. Late Afternoon the Next Day.

By the alley, Betty stands next to her large shopping cart filled with empties. She smokes a cigarette, head down, trying to be invisible.

    Out front, Wanda sits in her wheelchair, laser focused on sketching the trees and windows across the street on her large drawing pad. Wanda smokes a cigarette in an ornate cigarette holder. Next to her, Mateo sits on a milk crate, also drawing.

MATEO: . . . You need anything from the store, Miss Wanda?

WANDA WHEELS: No, dear.

MATEO: Cuz I could go for you.

WANDA WHEELS: There's nothing I require—except your company.

MATEO: Okay . . . Cuz I could go to Broadway right quick—or Amsterdam—

WANDA WHEELS: Your silent company.

MATEO: Silent. Yeah. Yeah I know . . . It's just, I just thought, like—

WANDA WHEELS: I'm hip to you, Mateo. I give you five dollars for hot cocoa, you come back with no change, wiping barbecue potato chip remains off your face—buttered roll in your back pocket, pack of Twinkies up your sleeve.

(Beat.)

MATEO: . . . I'm sorry, Miss Wanda.

WANDA WHEELS: Just draw, baby. Ain't a thing.

MATEO: Nah, but it is. I shouldn't do that. I'm sorry.

WANDA WHEELS: It's okay. I don't mind.

MATEO: . . . You don't?

WANDA WHEELS: I'm an adult. You're still a boy.

MATEO: Nah. That's not why . . . It's cuz you're kind.

(This concerns Wanda.)

WANDA WHEELS: Kind?! Is that what you go around telling people? That I'm kind?

MATEO: No.

WANDA WHEELS: You and me? We're compatible is all. I draw—you draw. I like quiet—and you mostly got the sense to know you haven't much to contribute by way of conversation. Don't pin a "kindness" target on me. There's a place for kindness. It's not here. This here's dog-eat-dog.

MATEO: I'm sorry, Miss Wanda—

WANDA WHEELS: Anybody ask you about me, tell 'em check the make and model: I'm a bitch on wheels.

(Beat . . . Then Mateo gets up to leave.)

Where you going? Sit down. Sit down and draw. Who you drawing today?

MATEO: . . . The Hulk versus General Thaddeus Thunderbolt Ross?

WANDA WHEELS: So—sit down. Give them life. Enjoy this last good light we got here.

(Mateo lingers, doesn't sit.)

MATEO: The truth is—it's embarrassing but—the truth is I'm hungry, Miss Wanda. I ain't eat today. I'm hungry.

WANDA WHEELS: Okay. Okay, young lord. I feel you. And Wanda got you. But you wanna be an artist, right?

MATEO: Yeah.

WANDA WHEELS: So put it on the paper . . . You're hungry— put it in that Hulk fella. Your shame, your anger—you are angry, right?

MATEO: Yeah.

WANDA WHEELS: Put it on the paper. Rage. Love. Pettiness. Kindness. That's the place. That's the safe place to have your feelings—not here. On the paper. Put it all on the paper.

(The door to the building entrance opens suddenly. Mobo shakes a finger at both Wanda and Betty.)

MR. MOBO: No smoking! And no smoking!

(Mobo notices Betty's shopping cart.)

That cart is yours, Betty Woods?

BETTY WOODS: Um, yeah?

MR. MOBO: You must remove it immediately. The neighbors, the block association, big trouble for us, no good.

(Mobo hands Wanda an Ensure protein shake.)

Drink it.

WANDA WHEELS: Non merci, mon frère. I am busy here—and I will not be force-fed like a late summer goose for autumn foie gras.

MR. MOBO: If you refuse, Rivera will send you back to the hospital. Mateo, make sure she drinks. I'll be right back.

(Mobo exits.)

MATEO: You gotta drink it, Miss Wanda. Mobo's right, you shriveling up to nothing, don't you wanna live?

(Wanda fishes ten dollars out of her purse. Offers it to Mateo.)

WANDA WHEELS: You drink it.

MATEO: Me?

WANDA WHEELS: C'mon, Mateo. Be quick. Take the money. Drink it.

MATEO: Nobody wants you to die, Miss Wanda.

WANDA WHEELS: I'll eat later. Now drink.

(Mateo takes the drink and guzzles it. It tastes nasty to him, but he drains it in one chug.)

Give it here.

*(Mateo gives her the empty carton. Wanda takes out a pint of vodka from her purse, fills the Ensure carton with vodka.
Mobo sticks his head out the door.)*

MR. MOBO: Are you drinking? This is a serious matter.

(Wanda raises the Ensure carton in a salute to Mobo, takes a long drink, makes a thing of exhaling after.)

WANDA WHEELS: Aaaaaaaaaaaaaaah. See?

MR. MOBO: Good girl. We want you healthy. So you can get out of that chair.

(Mobo pops back inside. Sugar and Munchies appear in work clothes. They're filthy and disheveled.)

QUEEN SUGAR: These motherfuckers!!!!!!!!!!!!!!!

WANDA WHEELS: What?

MUNCHIES: Community service!

QUEEN SUGAR: They axed us our preference! Our preference, mind you! We said Department of Parks, shit's across the street—or Goddard Riverside five blocks from here—

MUNCHIES: My aunt work there, they take care of us there—

QUEEN SUGAR: But these bitch-ass parole motherfuckers send us—to motherfuckin' JFK!

MUNCHIES: JFK!!!

MATEO: Airport?

MUNCHIES: Nah nigga, "JFK up the block"!! Dumbass, short-bus motherfucker—

WANDA WHEELS: Okay, okay—JFK for what?

QUEEN SUGAR: These tighty-whitey racist motherfuckers—and it *is* racism—

MUNCHIES: Zero white folk doing our job today—

WANDA WHEELS: Doing what?

QUEEN SUGAR: They had us dismantling homeless people's tents, trashing their shit! You know, motherfuckers be sleeping in the fields in back the airport again—

MUNCHIES: That shit was—I cried!

QUEEN SUGAR: She did!

MUNCHIES: And I ain't known for my empathy!

QUEEN SUGAR: Wanda—we homeless ourselves, parole people KNOW we homeless, and they INTENTIONALLY had us de-homing other homeless!

MUNCHIES: One little homeless fella—this man—he just had some garbage bags propped up on a stick, I ripped his shit down, and he was like, "But this my HOME! It's my HOME!" And he was serious! As if his shit was some real shit! And his shit wasn't shit, and he didn't hardly have shit, but still and all—it was his shit, ya know? Dat shit was his!

QUEEN SUGAR: Well, I need my shower now . . . They got hot water up in this bitch today?

MATEO: Boilers out.

QUEEN SUGAR: Again??? Oh, they fixing to close this place down, just watch.

MATEO: Miss Rivera was upstairs with the landlord and DHS before—

QUEEN SUGAR: See what I mean—pack your bags, y'all!

MATEO: Nah! City offered Miss Rivera a new job, Mobo said. "More money, less hours"—but Mobo said Miss Rivera said, "Fuck that," and Rosie said that means Miss Rivera's fighting for us—

QUEEN SUGAR: Yeah well, everybody got a price. Okay then—

WANDA WHEELS: We still on for later, Queenie?

QUEEN SUGAR: I'm sorry, I can't. I got my seminar tonight. I'm on the road to success now. I got you to thank for it. Lifting me up. My teacher, my guru . . . Mateo! When I'm out the shower, point me in the direction of who got that weed!

MATEO: I don't do that no more.

QUEEN SUGAR: Yeah, but you 411, so I know you know the nigga to be knowin'!

(Sugar enters the building as Rosie and Melba exit. They look like they've been crying.)

MUNCHIES: Y'all alright? Y'all look all shook.

LITTLE MELBA DIAZ: We just got out the AA meeting. You missed it!

MUNCHIES: And . . . ?

LITTLE MELBA DIAZ: I can't, but . . . shit was deep.

MUNCHIES: Deep how? . . . Rosie?

ROCKAWAY ROSIE: Oh no. No no no no no. I'm sorry. But when you see Sarge—

MUNCHIES: I'm waiting on her now.

ROCKAWAY ROSIE: Be, be, be—be nice to her. Poor dear, Be nice.

MUNCHIES: Nice?

LITTLE MELBA DIAZ: You know how Sarge don't never share at meetings but she been sober forever?

MUNCHIES: I mean, I don't follow that closely, I only go cuz I'm court ordered—

LITTLE MELBA DIAZ: Sarge fell off the wagon! I gotta get a new sponsor now! She drank last night, yo—

MUNCHIES: No.

LITTLE MELBA DIAZ: Yeah! All night and all alone. She and Bella had beef, Bella split, Sarge couldn't find her, Sarge lost it— she was still tipsy at the meeting!

MUNCHIES: What??!! Rosie?

(Rosie just shakes her head, waves Munchies away, and starts to cry.)

LITTLE MELBA DIAZ: And in the meeting? Sarge was—I mean it was so sad—

ROCKAWAY ROSIE: Sad!

LITTLE MELBA DIAZ: Hella sad. Hella hella. I couldn't look. But I heard. And I don't care—alcohol, PTSD, in-ebrified chronic manic panic—whatever—Sarge ain't going crunkadunk after ten years!

(Sarge exits from building all chipper, she seems perfectly normal, like too normal.)

Oh hey Sarge.

SARGE: What's up, yo?! Who gotta loosey for me?

MUNCHIES: Here ya go, Sarge.

SARGE: So what's the good word? . . . Wanda? You run over any puppies or little foo-foo white lady dogs today?

WANDA WHEELS: Nah, I steered clear.

SARGE: Y'all remember the time Wanda had that electric chair, she was a little tipsy, she ran over that bitch's dog?

(Munchies, Melba and Sarge laugh. Wanda just smiles, grits her teeth.)

MUNCHIES: That shit was too funny! What they call them dogs? Teacups?

LITTLE MELBA DIAZ: Shit-zoo! And then the lady, remember, she threaten to sue, and Miss Wanda said—whatchu said, Miss Wanda?

SARGE: Wanda went ghetto!

MUNCHIES: Wanda went all "Sarge" on her ass!

(They all laugh. Bella and Venus approach the entrance with Bella's baby carriage.

Bella is dressed nicely, in a conservative dress, with her hair done—a far cry from her usual "out-of-town junkie stripper ripped jeans and T-shirts." Venus is upgraded too, more proper and ladylike.

Sarge sees them and abruptly stops laughing. Then everybody stops laughing. Sarge takes a breath, smiles, acting nonchalant, but her blood is boiling.)

SARGE: Well, well, well. If it ain't "Wonder Woman" and "WonderWhatTheFuckYouStillDoingHere"!

VENUS RAMIREZ: All I'm doing here is the same thing you're doing.

SARGE: Yeah—looks like you moved right in.

BELLA: Oh come on! I couldn't find you this morning.

SARGE: Yeah? And I couldn't find you last *night*!!

ROCKAWAY ROSIE: Easy does it, Sarge.

SARGE: Oh I'm easy . . . But look at the two of y'all! All spiffy and deloused, lookin' all delightful an' shit—

BELLA: You're being an asshole.

VENUS RAMIREZ: We just went downtown.

SARGE: To do what—cop dope?!

BELLA: Venus took me to Federal Plaza to apply for housing! What is wrong with you?!

VENUS RAMIREZ: And for the record—I'm clean.

BELLA: And by the way—me and you just fuckin' met!

SARGE: Meaning what?

VENUS RAMIREZ: Please don't make a scene here Sarge, you'll wake the baby.

SARGE: "Wake the baby"?! What?! Like I'm an asshole who goes around waking babies?! You're Mrs. Fuckin' Doubtfire and you got a keen eye for baby wakers?!

BELLA: Let's go, Venus. *(To Sarge)* You need to check yourself, Sarge. You're behaving exactly like—this is exactly the situation I ran away from!

SARGE: But, Bella—I woulda took you to Federal Plaza!

BELLA: You been saying that for two weeks! You think I'm just gonna hang around here with you till you get your fuckin' shit together? I got Little Freddy to think of! And now—you're giving me even more I gotta think of! So you better reflect about where you're at and what you realistically have to offer—cuz this is—I've already done this, I've been doing endless variations of this since I woke up with tits—and I didn't come to New York City for another rerun of "let's play house with a broke-ass, emotionally unstable, obsessed, smothering narcissist," okay?! Because I'm a mother now, and I got plans, and dreams, and responsibilities, and I still got a shelf life—I'm not old like you—and

I got a right to aspire to, like—I don't know?!—normal?!—
or at least normal-ish?!—and I don't even know what that
is—but I want it—and I know it's not THIS—and on top
of the whole everything—I got my recovery to think of!

(Bella is exiting—)

SARGE: Recovery? Thirty-one days off the needle ain't nobody's
definition of recovery—and I ain't old! And I AM normal! And I certainly ain't no white-trash no-class stripper
neither!

(Bella is gone. Beat.)

MUNCHIES: . . . Fuck that ho, Sarge!

LITTLE MELBA DIAZ: Never liked her from the first beginning!

MUNCHIES: Skeezer tramp.

LITTLE MELBA DIAZ: Ratchet trick.

MUNCHIES: Bitch don't look that young to me!

LITTLE MELBA DIAZ: Bitch knew Burger King when nigga was
still the prince!

WANDA WHEELS: . . . Girls—maybe we need to give Sarge a little
privacy.

ROCKAWAY ROSIE: Privacy! Privacy, yes! Private time, private
moment, would you like some privacy, Sarge?

SARGE: I'm fine.

WANDA WHEELS: Okay then, Mateo and I were just headed for
the store.

MATEO: Store? Store, yeah. Store.

*(Mateo wheels Wanda up the block, passing Betty, and exiting.
Sarge notices Betty.)*

SARGE: Yo!!! That your cart?! Cart ain't supposed to be here!
Yo—you deaf?!

(Betty freezes, can't answer. Sarge ambles toward her. The others follow Sarge to Betty.
   Sarge gets close to Betty—)

I said is that—oh my God!!!

(Sarge coughs and grimaces, starts waving her hand around like she's trying to remove a foul odor.)

Guess you wasn't listening last night.

BETTY WOODS: . . . Listening?

SARGE: When I told you take a fuckin' shower!

BETTY WOODS: Oh. Oh, um—

SARGE: Cuz some peoples—actually a lot of peoples—in fact, all of us peoples—and more to the point, any motherfuckah with a sense of SMELL—any ANYBODY with the capacity to detect vile, foul, gag-inducing, horrifyingly offensive odor—we all might could easily interpret your overwhelmingly, stank-ti-fyingly foul, funk-i-fied stench as an act of *aggression*!

BETTY WOODS: It's not!

SARGE: See—no matter who any of us is, no matter race, color, or—in your case—diameter—the golden rule is we all gots to get along! Right, Rockaway?!

ROCKAWAY ROSIE: No! No! Don't put me in this, Sarge, no no, oh, no no—

SARGE: Rockaway Rosie here, she a straight-up Archie Bunker Bitch, if it was up to her, me and Munchies and Melba would be her slaves, peeling her powder-white ass some purple grapes off the vine—

ROCKAWAY ROSIE: No no, no vine! No vine, no slaves— No no Sarge, no slaves no politics—

SARGE: Rosie don't exactly like me—

ROCKAWAY ROSIE: No no. I like you very much, you're a real pip!

SARGE: Rosie don't really like none a us—

MUNCHIES: If Rosie ran the world—there'd only be like eight people!

ROCKAWAY ROSIE: No no! Oh no no no!

SARGE: But we don't fuck with Rosie—do we?

MUNCHIES: Rosie's down!

LITTLE MELBA DIAZ: That's my white granny homegirl right there!

SARGE: And we don't fuck with her—cuz the bitch KNOWS HOW TO GET ALONG!

MUNCHIES: She a get-along bitch—I grown fond of her!

SARGE: See—I been in every type of group dynamic from the Boogie Down Bronx to Iraq and Afghanistan—and the first rule of getting along is if you gonna be in close quarters— you best washing your Hind Quarters!! Wash yourself! Wash your nose and your toes—wash your pits and your tits! And ya better be goddamn sure to wash what?!

MUNCHIES: That motherfuckin' ass!

BETTY WOODS: I, I can't—

SARGE: Can't??!!

BETTY WOODS: My glands—I have a gland problem?

SARGE: Gland problem?!

BETTY WOODS: My glands, the water, I'll be covered in hives.

SARGE: Hives?! So we should have to suffer Armageddon of the Ass cuz you get—hives?! Your hive-free priority is more important than us choking to the point of asphyxiation and contracting toxic doody-booty stank syndrome?

(*Just then, Father Miguel approaches.*)

Morning, Padre.

| LITTLE MELBA DIAZ: Morning, Father. | MUNCHIES: Morning, Father. |

ROCKAWAY ROSIE: Morning, Father Miguel.

FATHER MIGUEL: Buenos dias, ladies. Miss Rivera in yet?

LITTLE MELBA DIAZ: Yes, Father.

FATHER MIGUEL: Say a prayer for Miss Rivera. Saints walk this earth. And that woman does more with less—and more for all of us—than you will ever know.

LITTLE MELBA DIAZ: But ain't saints supposed to smile once in a while?

(Father Miguel smiles broadly.)

FATHER MIGUEL: Saints toil. Buddhists smile.

(Father Miguel enters the building.)

SARGE: Okay—Rosie, watch the front door.

ROCKAWAY ROSIE: Oh no, no no no, please—I can't watch, and I won't, no no—I'm not, I won't, you know me, Sarge—oh no no no—

SARGE: Fine. Take Melba inside. Melba: Go study your books.

LITTLE MELBA DIAZ: But Sarge—

SARGE: Go!

(Rosie and Melba scurry off.)

MUNCHIES: All clear, Sarge.

(Betty starts to back away.)

BETTY WOODS: Please don't hurt me.

SARGE: Hurt you? I'm here to help you.

BETTY WOODS: You are?

SARGE: See, I got a military background.

BETTY WOODS: I support the troops!

SARGE: Shut the fuck up.

BETTY WOODS: I'll bathe I promise!

SARGE: Yesterday you got a warning. Today you get a lesson.

(Betty turns to run. Sarge grabs Betty by the throat. Betty is immobilized.)

You're lucky I'm back on my meds. Cuz I been known to lose control.

(Sarge applies pressure to Betty's neck and Betty falls to her knees. Sarge rears back to throw a vicious punch. Betty screams.)

SCENE 3

Miss Rivera's Office. Day.

Jennifer, a young social worker, and Rivera.

JENNIFER: They don't listen to me, Miss Rivera.

MISS RIVERA: Ms.

JENNIFER: What?

MISS RIVERA: Ms., not "miss." Continue.

JENNIFER: Sorry, the residents all call you miss.

MISS RIVERA: They call everybody miss. Go on—

JENNIFER: No, just, I try to do my job, they don't listen.

MISS RIVERA: And you want me to do what?

JENNIFER: I'm just telling you I come here every day, fully pre-
   pared, motivated—

MISS RIVERA: Maybe you need to go somewhere else.

JENNIFER: What?! But I just started two months ago! Look, I'm
   doing my best! But they just don't listen.

MISS RIVERA: Maybe you talk down to them.

JENNIFER: Talk down?! I could talk up, down, sideways, they don't listen. How can I do my job if they don't listen?!

(Suddenly, a quick knock on the door and the custodian, Joey, enters:)

JOEY FRESCO: Miss Rivera, sorry to disturb you, but cops are here.

MISS RIVERA: For what?

JOEY FRESCO: The new lady, you know, the big one?—they jumped her. Some of the ladies. Because she don't shower they say. The big one, I mean. They say she smell. So they jumped her.

So, the big one, she called 5-0. And they here.

MISS RIVERA: Where's Mister Mobo?

JOEY FRESCO: He talkin' to the cops. And big one ain't pressing charges. But Mobo said tell you what's up. And the big one—

MISS RIVERA: Betty Woods. That's her name.

JOEY FRESCO: The big one you mean?

MISS RIVERA: Yes. Put her on the third floor till things calm down. But she can't stay if she don't shower. Have Mobo tell her that, and tell Mobo come see me after.

JOEY FRESCO: After. Okay. Yes. Sorry.

(He exits and closes the door.)

MISS RIVERA: Look, I'll give you a letter of recommendation, you can use my name as a reference—

JENNIFER: I don't want a reference, I have a master's from Columbia, I owe a hundred fifty thousand dollars in student loans, I can't have gaps in my résumé—I don't know why you hired me if I'm being impeded from doing what you're paying me for!

MISS RIVERA: I didn't.

JENNIFER: Didn't what?

MISS RIVERA: Hire you. I didn't hire you. I'm underfunded, understaffed, the building's falling apart and I got more residents than beds—if I was allowed to do my own hiring, you think I would've chosen you? Even *you* wouldn't have chosen you.

JENNIFER: How about Jasmine then? Jasmine on the second floor started working here the same week as me. She just got her master's like I did. She's new at this like I am. She has problems with the residents like I do. But you help her. You visit her classroom. You tell the residents to show her respect. You bend over backwards for her. But never for me. I wonder why that is?

MISS RIVERA: Feel free to ponder that on your way out of my office.

JENNIFER: There's nothing to ponder. I know why. Manny the security guard told me. It's because I'm white.

MISS RIVERA: Manny told you that, huh?

JENNIFER: Just because I don't have shared cultural experiences with the residents—or you—doesn't mean I have nothing to contribute.

MISS RIVERA: Wow. Okay. Sorry it didn't work out for you here, please close the door on your way out.

JENNIFER: What?! Uh-uh, no way!

MISS RIVERA: "No way"? No way what?!

JENNIFER: I'm not quitting. I didn't come in here to quit. I'm not a quitter. So unless you're firing me—

MISS RIVERA: I'm firing you.

JENNIFER: What?

MISS RIVERA: You're fired.

JENNIFER: But—aren't we just talking?

MISS RIVERA: You're talking. I'm firing . . . You're fired, Jennifer. Good luck to you. Bye.

JENNIFER: . . . Oh . . . Um . . . Okay . . .

(Jennifer, shaken, starts to walk out, Rivera picks up the phone.)

MISS RIVERA: Miss Soto, call the plumbers again about the boiler—also—if there's still no forwarding address for that Jane Doe then her personal items need to be disposed of. Which reminds me—

(Jennifer heads back to Rivera's desk—)

Never mind I'll call you back. *(To Jennifer)* What?

JENNIFER: I don't want to be fired. I came to your office because I needed help, but I didn't ask you because I was afraid—so I barged in and just kinda complained, and got defensive—and then, you know—ascended the highest peak of Mount Fucking Jackass by accusing you of racism—because bosses love that—and even though I know full well racism is a system of oppression—and that people of color cannot by design ever benefit from that system, and therefore by definition, people of color can't be racists—although—I mean, I do sometimes think that's kind of a little bit bullshit sometimes, or, like—linguistics, semantics—even though I know that me dismissing it as such—even just occasionally, is really a reflexive exercise in privilege on my part—an escape hatch from acknowledging the obvious societal advantage my color and class afford me—and, um, um, oh wow—I'm sorry, I'm totally lost—

MISS RIVERA: What do you want, Jennifer?

JENNIFER: I get that I'm fired, Ms. Rivera—and I deserve it, and I'm a total idiot, but I love it here, I love this, and I'm so sorry, and I know I gave you no choice, but I just want to help, and—I can do this, I know it. It's all I've ever wanted to do. And I just wish I could help. Because I wanna help.

(Beat.)

MISS RIVERA: Fine . . . Go do that then.

JENNIFER: . . . What?

MISS RIVERA: Help. You want to help? Then go help somebody. You want me to give you the answers? Here's the answers: The residents will not trust you if you don't come correct. So never pretend you're someone you're not—they see right through that. Don't lie to them—they always know. Don't act tougher than you are, they'll call your bluff. Don't patronize them—that's the story of their life. Check your privilege and your assumptions and your neurosis at the door. Don't beg. Don't scold. Don't pose. Just help one of them. If they won't listen to you, find the one person who's trying to listen, there's always one, and go help her. Give her your time. Be of help. The others will notice. Now go.

JENNIFER: Thank you.

(Jennifer offers her hand to Rivera, who ignores it.)

MISS RIVERA: One more thing: Dress down. Use less products. Don't no one want help from some bougie Peppermint Patty. Get out of my office.

(Jennifer exits. Rivera picks up her phone—)

Miss Soto? Send that fuckin' Manny Diaz from security up to my office right away, please? And tell him to bring his keys and his time card.

(Rivera opens her desk, takes out a half-pint bottle, takes a swig— then puts the bottle back in her desk and pops a stick of gum in her mouth, as—
Door knocks and opens. A young man, Mateo, enters.)

MATEO: Miss Rivera? Munchies said I could ax you for some socks cuz you might have some? Like tube socks? Or even any socks? I like tube socks—but even black socks, or other dress socks, thermal-type socks, even ankle socks, or them diabetes socks, whatever socks I can get cuz I really need 'em. Socks, I mean.

MISS RIVERA: Mateo, did you hear me say, "Come in"?

MATEO: You mean when I knocked?

MISS RIVERA: When you knocked, yes.

MATEO: Um, no.

MISS RIVERA: Okay then—go back outside try again.

MATEO: Knock on the door again? Oh, okay . . .

(He exits. Then knocks.)

MISS RIVERA: I'm busy come back later!

MATEO: . . . Oh . . . Oh, okay.

(Beat. Rivera sighs, picks up phone.)

MISS RIVERA: Miss Soto, call my daughter, would ya? Have her come in, give her pizza money, I'm staying late. And the plastic sheets for the fifth floor yes, tell Hernando. Yes, I'm authorizing it. Oh—and Miss Soto? You know the resident on seven, in the infirmary, on dialysis, early onset dementia, the one she doesn't speak? Perez, yes! Marisol Perez. Great. Okay. Her son needs socks, can we find him some? Yes, "the smoothed-face boy," that's him. Okay. Okay—

(The door knocks.)

One moment! Miss Soto, I gotta go.

(Door knocks again. Rivera hangs up phone. Sighs.)

Come in. Hello? I said come in!

(Door opens as lights fade.)

SCENE 4

An Unexpected Evening Visitor.

In the community room, Father Miguel, stripped of his shirt and collar, is leading Mateo, Melba and Munchies through a set of basic tai chi poses.

Outside, Sonia and Taina sit on the steps waiting on a food delivery. Sonia is annoyed. Taina plays Ms. Pac-Man on her cell phone.

HAPPY MEAL SONIA: Call them again!

TAINA: Ma, I just called!

HAPPY MEAL SONIA: Then call them again!

TAINA: But I just called!

(Sonia tries to grab the phone from her.)

HAPPY MEAL SONIA: ¡Dame el teléfono! ¡Respetame! ¡Dame! ¡¡DAME!!

(Sonia slaps Taina upside the head and takes her phone.)

TAINA: Ow! Ma!

(Just then a man—Nicky—begins approaching the building. Sonia's mood immediately brightens.)

HAPPY MEAL SONIA: Oh, baby girl, look—he's here! *(To Nicky)* Yoo-hoo! Two cheeseburger deluxe with disco fries and a rice pudding. Sonia Figueroa. You're Grubhub, right?

NICKY: Uh, no.

(Nicky steps over them and enters the building. Sonia is crestfallen.)

HAPPY MEAL SONIA: Ay Nena, I thought he was Grubhub.

(Taina puts her arm around Sonia to comfort her.)

TAINA: White people don't deliver Grubhub in Manhattan, Ma . . .

(Inside the building, Nicky is strutting past Father Miguel and the others, heading for an upstage door. Father Miguel grabs his shirt and collar and hustles to place his body in between Nicky and his destination.)

FATHER MIGUEL: Can I help you?

NICKY: Nah, I'm good.

(Nicky attempts a step forward. Father Miguel takes a step back, but maintains his position blocking the door.)

FATHER MIGUEL: Sorry, no visitors.

NICKY: I'm here to see my wife.

FATHER MIGUEL: Sorry. That's not allowed.

NICKY: Not allowed? She's my wife. You got a wife?

FATHER MIGUEL: No sir, I don't . . . Now please, building's closed.

NICKY: Building's closed? I took two subways and a fuckin' express bus to get here!

FATHER MIGUEL: Mateo. Take the girls and go upstairs.

MATEO: But I got your back, Father—

FATHER MIGUEL *(To Melba and Munchies)*: Ladies. Go with Mateo. *(To Mateo)* Mateo: Go.

MATEO: But Father—

FATHER MIGUEL: Now.

(They exit. Father Miguel stares down Nicky.)

NICKY: Do I smell bad or something? Cuz I'm not here to make trouble, Father—

FATHER MIGUEL: Let's talk outside.

NICKY: Yeah see, I already been outside. Now I'm inside. And I don't really need to talk, but if you wanna talk, we can talk right here—can't we?

FATHER MIGUEL: Outside is better.

NICKY: Better for you maybe—but for me—

FATHER MIGUEL: Your wife filed a restraining order. I could have you arrested—

NICKY: See, that don't sound like her—

FATHER MIGUEL: It's time for you to go—

NICKY: Okay, enough with the face and the commands already. Me and my wife: We're Catholics, Father. Mass every Sunday, confession, bingo, never turned down a raffle ticket in my life—

FATHER MIGUEL: I was present when your wife was admitted. She was beaten half to death.

NICKY: She fell!

FATHER MIGUEL: You need to leave.

NICKY: What? You calling me a liar?! She fell!! She's always falling!! She's a fuckin' drunk, okay?! We got three kids, I can't trust her to take care of them, she's half in the bag before dinner!

FATHER MIGUEL: Outside.

NICKY: "Outside," sure. Like she's the victim! Well what about her hitting me?! You see this? From my wife! This one? Also my wife! She acts all innocent but she's a fuckin' animal!

FATHER MIGUEL: Lower your voice.

NICKY: Or what?! Jesus Christ, you're getting me all riled up here, I was calm when I came in—I was calm!!

(Nicky pulls a pint from his back pocket and takes a big swig.)

FATHER MIGUEL: Let's talk outside. We have a domestic violence program for perpetrators in Brooklyn—I could get you in.

NICKY: *Perpetrator??!!* I'm not a fuckin' *perpetrator*! I'm a Roman Catholic and a union man! I pay my taxes, the mortgage, my kids have everything, good to my in-laws—my yard's fuckin' impeccable—I'm a sucker for anybody lookin' for a handout—bums on the street, those late-night infomercials on TV— *Perpetrator?!!*— If I'm a perpetrator that the world needs more of—I mean, who the fuck are you to call me that??!!

FATHER MIGUEL: Let's go—

(Father Miguel attempts to escort Nicky out; Nicky smacks Father Miguel's hands away—)

NICKY: You better watch yourself! My bride is upstairs. My girl! And nobody knows what goes on behind closed doors! Not you! Not nobody!

FATHER MIGUEL: I'm going to invite you one more time to leave—now.

NICKY: Okay. Cards on the table: Look here, faggot. You think I'm afraid to hit some midget homo spic priest?! Like I'm afraid God's gonna turn me into a pillar of dust—or a fuckin' whatever, a paralyzed cockroach with no legs and fuckin' leukemia or some shit?! Fuck you—God ain't here and you ain't special!

(Nicky rushes Father Miguel, attempting to go upstairs. Father Miguel steps back, flattens him. Father Miguel steps on his neck, slowly applying pressure, cutting off Nicky's breathing.)

FATHER MIGUEL: Like I said before: We have a domestic violence program for perpetrators in Brooklyn—I could get you in.
NICKY: Fuck off!
FATHER MIGUEL: Or I could call the cops.
NICKY: Fuck you!
FATHER MIGUEL: Or I could keep applying pressure to your windpipe—like this—until it cracks in two, or you asphyxiate yourself—
NICKY: Fuck you, fuck y— Hey, hey stop! Stop! Hey, ya fuckin' crazy?! Stop!!!

(Father Miguel stares him down, slowly releasing the tension on Nicky's windpipe. Nicky chokes, coughs . . . then starts to cry.)

. . . I want my wife. Please. I love my wife. Please, please, I'll do anything—anything—

(Father Miguel helps Nicky to his feet.)

She's gonna be okay though, right? Can you just tell her I'm sorry? You can see I'm sorry, right? Right? Oh God. Oh God you shoulda just snapped my neck off.

(Father Miguel escorts Nicky out the door.)

FATHER MIGUEL: There's a diner down up the block. If you wait for me there, I'll take you to Brooklyn later.

NICKY: To what—the violence program? I mean—does that shit actually work?

FATHER MIGUEL: Not always. But sometimes . . . It worked for me.

NICKY: You?

FATHER MIGUEL: Yeah.

NICKY *(Referring to Father Miguel's attack on him)*: You sure about that?

FATHER MIGUEL: If you're at the diner, I'll take you to Brooklyn.

(Rivera exits the building.)

MISS RIVERA: Miguel! What's going on here, and all the yelling?! Who is this?!

FATHER MIGUEL: It's okay. He's leaving.

MISS RIVERA *(To Nicky)*: Okay, well whoever you are, move it up the block and don't come back or we'll have you arrested.

(Nicky exits.)

FATHER MIGUEL: He was just—

MISS RIVERA: I don't wanna know. Goodnight.

(Father Miguel reenters building. Outside, Rivera sees Sonia and Taina, and approaches them.)

Hi, ladies. What are you doing?

HAPPY MEAL SONIA: Waiting for Grubhub. But it never came. Taina, call them again.

MISS RIVERA: Sonia. Over here. If you go inside and ask Father Miguel, Miss Soto made a pernil and mofongo for the staff today, and there's leftovers.

HAPPY MEAL SONIA: Oh! Thank you, Miss Rivera. Come on, Taina.

MISS RIVERA: I need to talk to your daughter.

HAPPY MEAL SONIA: Okay, but Taina will come after, right?

TAINA: I'll be right in, Ma.

HAPPY MEAL SONIA: Okay. I know how you like mofongo!

(She exits.)

TAINA: Am I in trouble?

MISS RIVERA: I don't know. What'd you do?

TAINA: Nothing, miss.

MISS RIVERA: I doubt that. Here.

(Rivera hands Taina a manila envelope.)

TAINA: What's this?

MISS RIVERA: The archdiocese gives away full scholarships each year as part of their Second Chance Program. You studied culinary arts at Manhattan Vocational High School—

TAINA: But that was a long time ago—I'm twenty-five now, miss.

MISS RIVERA: Like I said it's called the Second Chance Program. There's a school upstate in Utica—you could go there, get a degree, become certified as a chef, or in hospitality, make good money, plus benefits. Your transcripts suggest you have the aptitude, so I nominated you—anyway, it's all in the envelope there with the application.

TAINA: And my moms could come too?

MISS RIVERA: No.

TAINA: Oh, well then, thank you, miss, but we'll just stay here.

MISS RIVERA: Taina. We can no longer provide adequate care for your mother.

TAINA: But she don't need much, miss. And me neither.

MISS RIVERA: Her spells and mood swings are increasing, she's getting worse—

TAINA: She's fine.

MISS RIVERA: She's not taking her meds—the risperidone, the Depakote—

TAINA: She takes them!

MISS RIVERA: Taina.

TAINA: I mean, she tries, but the antipsychotics make her vomit and be asleep, and the bipolar pills make her fat and she be losing her hair, miss—

MISS RIVERA: She belongs in a hospital.

TAINA: She won't go.

MISS RIVERA: She needs a CAT scan.

TAINA: For what?

MISS RIVERA: The MS. C'mon, Taina, this isn't new.

TAINA: She's fine.

MISS RIVERA: She's not.

TAINA: I'm the one who's with her. I'm the one sleeps with her, eats with her, does everything with her—she don't have no MS!

MISS RIVERA: Are you a doctor?

TAINA: Fuck you, miss! You wanna put us on the street—fine. But she ain't going to no hospital, and I ain't abandoning her for nothing!

MISS RIVERA: Taina—you are a good daughter. You love your mother.

TAINA: And she loves me!

MISS RIVERA: Okay—but she's sick. Very sick. Because if she wasn't sick, Taina—she would never let you carry this weight.

TAINA: I ain't carrying—

MISS RIVERA: I have a daughter, Taina. I'm here eighty hours a week, I hardly see her—so my mothering, in the few moments a day I actually get to spend with her, is all about giving her wings. Not chains. Wings. Good mothers do that. Your mom can't do it, it's not her fault. So you gotta do it for her. And for yourself.

TAINA: Myself?! I don't even know who that is, miss. My mother suffered in her life, okay? Suffered and suffered and she needs me!! And she ain't like how you all think! And even if she is—nah. Nah, fuck that! And fuck you, miss. Fuck you!

SCENE 5

Group Therapy in the Community Room. Mid-Session.

Group therapy with Jennifer. Taina's upset. Sonia is alert and atten-
tive. Rosie too. Wanda is drunk, sleeping. Melba organizing her book
bag, but attentive. Munchies bored as hell. Bella with headphones
on—she and Sugar are writing notes and passing pamphlets back and
forth and seem to be in a low-key disagreement. But all eyes are on—

TAINA: C'mon, miss! How many more times I gotta fuckin' say
it?! Where my mother goes, I go! We ain't separating for
nobody—we Siamese Twins of the Heart! Y'all wanna put
her in Bellevue? Put me there too! You wanna let me stay
here? Then she gonna stay here too! We here for housing,
not this bullshit . . . Cuz I mean, you think I'm unaware
of my situation? You think I don't know, like, other girls,
like, you know, whatever, and that maybe it'd be—different

if it was different? Well it ain't. And it never fucking was. Never. So just—okay? She's my mother. I ain't never gonna leave her behind.

JENNIFER: . . . Rosie?

ROCKAWAY ROSIE: Oh, no no no no. Just—I—took care of my, took care of my mother. I did that. But I never had the opportunity, um, I wasn't blessed with the good fortune to be a parent, so, I can't, I mean, the other side of it, I really can't say—not that I would say—but I guess if I had to say—oh who cares what the hell I have to say—but, uh, I am, well—the benefit of age, oh never mind. But I respect Taina for what she's doing. Sonia too, of course, but uh— no no no no—yeah, uh, no—yeah no that's all.

(Rosie wells up, blows her nose.)

JENNIFER: Sonia—how do you feel about all this?

HAPPY MEAL SONIA: Oh . . . Well, I feel Taina should be free.

TAINA: No you don't!

HAPPY MEAL SONIA: I tell her all the time I'll be fine any old place, she needs to live her life—but my daughter's stubborn. And she loves me too much. Because I protected her, she wants to protect me, because I sacrificed everything for her, and for my own mother too, but, I was raised like that, you know, to do what's right? But now, it's modern times, so just because I made those sacrifices for her—I understand why she don't always wanna do the same—

TAINA: Ma, I've made sacrifices—

JENNIFER: Like your scholarship application? Did you finish writing it? Or is that something you're willing to throw away?

HAPPY MEAL SONIA: Scholarship?

TAINA: It's nothing, Ma.

JENNIFER: Taina has a chance to go away and study for free.

HAPPY MEAL SONIA: Go away and leave me?! No! No no! She don't wanna!

JENNIFER: Bella—Bella, Sugar, hey! Is that a conversation you can share with the group?

BELLA: It's not me! She's trying to sell me fuckin' Amway!

QUEEN SUGAR: This ain't Amway!

BELLA: My stepmother used to sell Amway back in Baltimore, okay? I'm hip to Amway—

QUEEN SUGAR: But this ain't Amway!

BELLA: It's a pyramid thing—it's Amway!

JENNIFER: Okay, can we put our attention on Taina—she may need help with a decision—

QUEEN SUGAR: Taina? I already tried to help her ass last week!

TAINA: How? By trying to sell me that Amway crap?

QUEEN SUGAR: It ain't Amway!

TAINA: She tried to sell Rosie too, right, Rosie?

ROCKAWAY ROSIE: Oh no no no no—I mean, well, yes—but, Sugar means well—

QUEEN SUGAR: Thank you!—

ROCKAWAY ROSIE: She doesn't realize it's—"hinky."

QUEEN SUGAR: It ain't hinky, Rosie!

LITTLE MELBA DIAZ: What's "hinky"? (To Munchies) Like janky?!

MUNCHIES: Nah, janky like janky—hinky like, I dunno, some white shit.

BELLA: It's fraud.

LITTLE MELBA DIAZ: Oh! Like wangboozling!

QUEEN SUGAR: It ain't no wangboozle! And it ain't no fraud!

TAINA: It's a scam!

BELLA: It's fuckin' Amway!

QUEEN SUGAR: You know what? All a y'all ain't never gonna amount to nuthin cuz y'all ignorant—the whole lot of you! "FAM-WAY" is NOT "AmWay." FAM-WAY is about family! Which is why I'm trying to help you motherfuckers, cuz I see you as family! Fam-Way has a positive vision—

and that vision is played out daily as Fam-Way helps people everywhere discover their potential and achieve their goals by offering great brands and opportunities.

BELLA: Sounds like Amway.

QUEEN SUGAR: Well it's fuckin' not, ya dumb, out-of-town bitch! Miss Jennifer: Fam-Way is guided by the core Fam-Way values: Partnership, Integrity, Personal Worth, Achievement, Personal Responsibility and Free Enterprise.

JENNIFER: I see, but—

BELLA: Amway.

QUEEN SUGAR: It's not Amway!!!

BELLA: Okay, fine. But it's fuckin' Amway.

QUEEN SUGAR: It ain't.

BELLA: Amway.

QUEEN SUGAR: Nope!

BELLA: Amway!

(Sugar rises—)

QUEEN SUGAR: Say "Amway" one more time! Go ahead, bitch, say it!

JENNIFER: Sugar! Sugar, please!

(Just then, Sarge saunters in.)

SARGE: S'up, Sugar—what's good?

(Sugar sits back down, reorganizing her Fam-Way brochures.)

QUEEN SUGAR: Aw, you know, Sarge: Give a bitch a fish, she'll eat for a day. Teach a bitch to fish—but some bitches don't never want to learn.

(Sarge goes to sit down next to Bella. Bella quickly rises, walks across the room to sit on the other side. The room grows tense. Melba see this, quickly goes through her book bag.)

LITTLE MELBA DIAZ: Hey Sarge—would you like a goat pencil
case?

HAPPY MEAL SONIA: I'd like a goat pencil case!

LITTLE MELBA DIAZ: Here you go. And one for you, Sarge—and
Rosie—

SARGE: Thanks, Melba—

ROCKAWAY ROSIE: Oh, and I can put my toiletries in here! Oh,
and it's so cute—look Sarge, with the goats—thank you,
Melba! Oh—how much do I owe you?

LITTLE MELBA DIAZ: Na, don't worry, Rosie—it was free—

HAPPY MEAL SONIA: Free from where?!

LITTLE MELBA DIAZ: Here ya go, Miss Jennifer. From my summer school. We visited the goats today.

MUNCHIES: Goats where? Ain't no goats—you mean the zoo?

JENNIFER: Uptown, right?

HAPPY MEAL SONIA: Uptown?

LITTLE MELBA DIAZ: In the park there. Riverside. By Grant's
Tomb. They got some infestation of weeds or vegetation—

MUNCHIES: Vegetation?

LITTLE MELBA DIAZ: Like hazardous, yeah—and it's easier for
goats to eat it then for humans to do the job, so they got
goats there now, with names and personalities, and they
going back home soon, but they been here all summer eating up all the bad weeds and vegetation for us, and we went
and they gave us free stuff and it was cool.

HAPPY MEAL SONIA: Isn't that nice, Taina?

TAINA: Yeah, Ma, it's real nice.

HAPPY MEAL SONIA: Are you taking a tone with me?

TAINA: I'm not taking no fuckin' tone, Ma.

HAPPY MEAL SONIA: Yeah, but you took that application, didn't
you?

TAINA: . . . Ma, I didn't even fill it out.

HAPPY MEAL SONIA: Then give it to me.

TAINA: Ma!

HAPPY MEAL SONIA: So you did fill it out.

TAINA: I didn't fill it out!

HAPPY MEAL SONIA: Then where is it?

JENNIFER: Sonia—

HAPPY MEAL SONIA: Where is it?!

TAINA: Jesus fuckin' Christ, Ma!

(Taina rises, storms out of the room. Sonia races after her—)

HAPPY MEAL SONIA: Taina! Baby, wait!

(Sonia stops a moment to address Jennifer:)

Sneaky cunt! Rich bitch whore! You gonna see what's gonna happen to you! Santera! Santera!
    (To Taina) Taina! Baby, I'm sorry! Taina!

(Sonia runs out and exits. Jennifer is a bit shaken up.)

JENNIFER: Wow . . . Let's break for today.

(Everyone is still a little in shock. Munchies breaks the tension doing her Exorcist *voice—)*

MUNCHIES: "Sneaky vagina"! "Santera santera"! Sugar, Melba, let's go to bodega! Wanda slept through that shit, I'll wheel her to her room!!!

(Munchies and the others laugh. Munchies wheels Wanda out. Everyone exits. Bella and Sarge are alone.)

SARGE: . . . Bella.

BELLA: I don't wanna talk to you.

SARGE: Where you going?

BELLA: Smoke.

SARGE: Can I come wit' you?

(Bella exits toward outside the building, Sarge following.)

BELLA: If I say no, you going to beat me up? Like you did to that poor heavyset woman?

SARGE: What? Bella. Bella. I didn't do nothing.

BELLA: Everybody knows about it. And about you drinking again?!

SARGE: Already got two days back.

BELLA: Do you have any idea how that makes me feel? We have a fight, Carmen—then you pick up and it's because of me?! I can't carry that! You're supposed to be the strong one, the rock—now I've got more clean days than you?!

SARGE: Baby—

(Just then, they bump into Father Miguel and Mateo with fishing rods and buckets.)

FATHER MIGUEL: Ladies. Good afternoon.

SARGE: Afternoon, Father. Y'all been fishing?

FATHER MIGUEL: Hudson River. We did pretty well.

(Mateo flashes his bucket at Bella.)

MATEO: Look, Bella—eels!!!

BELLA: Waaaaaaah! Fuck!!!! . . . Fuckin' shit! Fuck! Shit. Shit . . . I'm sorry, Father.

(Father Miguel, Sarge and Mateo laugh.)

FATHER MIGUEL *(To Bella)*: You're new here. And don't worry—I was a merchant marine.

BELLA: I'm just, I'm not used to priests. And kids. With fucking eels!

MATEO: My bad, Bella. My bad, Sarge.

SARGE: Get on out of here.

(As Father Miguel and Mateo exit—)

MATEO: Father, the game, the Mets game, Father—it starts at 7:30.

FATHER MIGUEL: Yes I know, Mateo—you've already mentioned it five times.

(They exit. Bella and Sarge are alone.)

SARGE: Bella . . . I fucked up. Then I fucked up again. Then I really fucked up. Then I fucked up in public, talking bad to you out here, I shouldn't never have done that. And to that dude Venus too. We got beef, me and him—and the Big Book says, "People, Places, and Things," Bella, but I trust you, and it seem like y'all get along and I ain't gonna fuck with that. I promise.

BELLA: And she's a woman, Carmen.

SARGE: Um . . . Okay, that's gonna take me a minute, but, okay. Anyway . . . after I disrespected you out here yesterday, in front of folks, I fucked up again. That Betty Woods, she's not supposed to smell like that, it's actually a rule, but I hit her—I hit her because I was so angry—because—I was so afraid—afraid of losing you—

BELLA: I think we need to take a step back——

SARGE: I don't wanna. I will if you wanna—but I don't wanna. I love you.

BELLA: You don't know me. And believe me, if you did know me, like really know me, or even if you just knew me a little more than you do right now, trust me—

SARGE: Nah. I love you, Bella. I got some issues, you've seen all of them now—including some I didn't even know I had. But that's all of them. I swear. And I am older than you and I don't have it like that yet to treat you how I wanna, I mean financially, you and Little Freddy, but I heard what you said, about being normal, and I want that, I wanted that the very first second I laid eyes on you. I been around. I'm not stupid. You been around a little too.

BELLA: More than a little—

SARGE: Look at me. You see me? Put your hand—here, right here on my heart. You feel that?

BELLA: I do.

SARGE: I commanded a platoon. I survived combat. Kept my people safe. Took care of the villagers as much as I could. I looked death in the eye—twice—and I didn't flinch. I can do this, Bella. I can do this with you. If you let me. I can do this. It's all I want. And we could go slow. I will provide for you and for Little Freddy. How about you give me a chance.

BELLA: I don't know.

SARGE: Gimme a chance.

BELLA: It's gotta be slow.

SARGE: Gimme a chance.

BELLA: I feel what you feel. I do. But—

SARGE: Gimme a chance.

BELLA: Don't do that. We're, it's public.

SARGE: Modest stripper.

BELLA: I'm shy inside. I'm shy. And I'm not a sure bet. I'm not.

SARGE: Gimme a chance.

BELLA: Baby. Baby stop it.

SARGE: Gimme a chance.

BELLA: You're bad.

SARGE: Gimme a chance.

BELLA: I'll tell you what.

SARGE: What?

BELLA: I might give you a chance.

SARGE: Oh yeah?

BELLA: But first, you gotta give me—a kiss.

(They kiss. They're kissing.)

I want ice cream.

SARGE: I know a place.

(They kiss, walk down the block, exit.)

SCENE 6

Common Area. Night.

Upstage, Betty sits alone scribbling in her journal. She has a black eye and bruises and welts.

Downstage, Venus and Joey spill out of the broom closet, quickly pulling up panties and buckling belts. They take no notice of Betty, as—

VENUS RAMIREZ: Sixty dollars—

JOEY FRESCO: Ay—pero, mami—

VENUS RAMIREZ: "Ay pero, mami" nada! Sixty dollars!

JOEY FRESCO: But I'm saying—

VENUS RAMIREZ: ¡Hijo de puta barato! Sixty dollars! ¡Sesenta dólares! ¡Coño!

JOEY FRESCO: But we do this all the time!

VENUS RAMIREZ: Sí—for sixty dollars!

JOEY FRESCO: But, c'mon, we got feelings, maybe it started as a john to ho—

VENUS RAMIREZ: Who you callin' a ho?

JOEY FRESCO: See? Dass right! You ain't no ho! And if you ain't no ho, then why I gotta pay for? Cuz, baby, in my heart, and in my all over, I consider this a real relationship.

VENUS RAMIREZ: Oh we in a relationship?

JOEY FRESCO: Yeah, I mean I see you more than—

VENUS RAMIREZ: Your wife?

JOEY FRESCO: She just my wife for the papers, I told you—

VENUS RAMIREZ: Ay, macho, por favor: You got a wife, two baby mommas, five kids, plus that Ecuadorian "Reina Gorda de Montaña Fea" bitch in Corona—and—you still fuckin' that little negrita from the Duane Reade right up the damn block—so tell me more, papi—about how this is a real relationship—

JOEY FRESCO: Because I think about you when you're not around. Okay? In my private thoughts, baby.

VENUS RAMIREZ: If this is a real relationship, introduce me to your kids.

(Joey sighs, opens his wallet, goes to hand her money, then wags his finger at her.)

JOEY FRESCO: I'm sincere. You'll see.

VENUS RAMIREZ: Cash, bitch.

(Suddenly, as Joey hands her the money, he notices Betty staring at them.
He whispers:)

JOEY FRESCO: Uh-oh. She sees us.

VENUS RAMIREZ: Who?

JOEY FRESCO: The big one. You think she'd tell?

(Just then, Melba enters—)

LITTLE MELBA DIAZ: Mister Joey! Miss Rivera said go to the cafeteria, someone left something there.

JOEY FRESCO: Left what?

LITTLE MELBA DIAZ: She didn't say.

JOEY FRESCO: Okay.

(Joey grabs his mop and rolling bucket, and exits.)

LITTLE MELBA DIAZ: It was ca-ca they left. You know, like—from a human?

(Melba runs off. From across the room, Venus studies Betty, sees her wounds.)

VENUS RAMIREZ: Excuse me, miss: Who did that to you?

BETTY WOODS: Nobody.

VENUS RAMIREZ: You know, they gonna hurt you bad if you don't bathe.

BETTY WOODS: That's okay. I'm not staying.

VENUS RAMIREZ: Yeah? Where you going?

BETTY WOODS: I don't know.

(Venus crosses to her, looks through her bag, pulls out some cheap perfume spray. Shows it to Betty.)

VENUS RAMIREZ: May I?

(Venus sprays Betty's wrists, neck, behind her ears.)

BETTY WOODS: You don't have to be nice to me.

VENUS RAMIREZ: Oh I'm not being nice. If they fuck you up bad, the police will come—and I got warrants.

(Venus finishes spraying, hands Betty the bottle.)

Keep it.

(Venus walks off.)

BETTY WOODS: Thank you.
VENUS RAMIREZ: Stay there. I'll be back.

SCENE 7

Mr. Mobo's Bedroom. Night.

Munchies having sex with Mobo.

MR. MOBO: We can't do this anymore.

MUNCHIES: I know, Mister Mobo. Don't stop.

MR. MOBO: This is not proper.

MUNCHIES: Not proper at all—a scandal.

MR. MOBO: A scandal—yes.

MUNCHIES: Oooh! Ooh! Hit it hard, Africa!

MR. MOBO: I'm hitting it. Yes I am. But I feel God will punish me. And definitely Miss Rivera!

MUNCHIES: Oooh! Ooh! You're such a nerd-ass, but you fuck like the truth.

MR. MOBO: The truth, yes. Oh God the truth!

MUNCHIES: Oooh! Ooh! Ooh!

(When suddenly a knock at the door—)

HAPPY MEAL SONIA: Mister Mobo? Mister Mobo, hello?

MR. MOBO: Oh no. We must stop. Please stop.

MUNCHIES: I'll bite the pillow, but don't you stop!

HAPPY MEAL SONIA: Mister Mobo, you said I could come see you?

MR. MOBO: Yes, yes, one minute!

HAPPY MEAL SONIA: Mister Mobo, I'm afraid I'm losing my daughter, Mister Mobo. I feel her moving away from me. Can you hear me? Mister Mobo? Mister Mobo?

MR. MOBO: Yes, dear, I hear you. Listen, I am ill. I cannot come to the door. But your daughter, she loves you. Maybe get her a gift to show you care. Something you know she would love.

HAPPY MEAL SONIA: She loves animals.

MR. MOBO: Good. A stuffed animal, yes!

HAPPY MEAL SONIA: Not real?

MR. MOBO: Well, real or stuffed, whatever suits you.

HAPPY MEAL SONIA: Yes! Yes! I know just the thing! Thank you, Mister Mobo! You are one of God's chosen!

(Sonia leaves. They continue fucking.)

MR. MOBO: God's chosen yes. Chosen for Hell!

SCENE 8

The Bathroom. Evening.

In a soapy tub sits Betty, weeping. Behind her, Venus scrubs her with a big brush.

BETTY WOODS: I'm so sorry.
VENUS RAMIREZ: Arm!

    (Betty lifts her arm. Venus scrubs it.)

BETTY WOODS: This must be awful for you . . .
VENUS RAMIREZ: Other arm!

    (Betty lifts her other arm. Venus scrubs. Betty weeps.)

BETTY WOODS: I'm so sorry. You're so kind.

VENUS RAMIREZ: Shut up. In Puerto Rico, I used to do this for my tia. She was like you. I know why you don't bathe. You don't wanna show yourself.

(Betty weeps and nods.)

Even to yourself.

(Betty weeps and nods more.)

And that's bullshit. You're beautiful.
BETTY WOODS: I'm not.
VENUS RAMIREZ: Like Lana Turner.
BETTY WOODS: I bear no resemblance to Lana Turner.
VENUS RAMIREZ: Hey. Stay still.

(Venus washes Betty's hair.)

Shame on you discounting yourself. With this thick wavy hair, your pale blue eyes, alabaster skin like royalty—
BETTY WOODS: Oh stop it!
VENUS RAMIREZ: You have to love yourself, girl. Your whole self. You ain't just a head. You a body. You gotta love all of it.
BETTY WOODS: Yeah, sure. Easy for you to say!
VENUS RAMIREZ: Oh yeah? Easy for me to say why?
BETTY WOODS: Because you know . . .
VENUS RAMIREZ: No I don't know.
BETTY WOODS: Because you're thin, okay?! That's why it's easy for you! Try being me, asshole! Try being me for even one day and you'd slit your wrists!

(Venus stops washing Betty. She rises, pulls the sleeves on her dress.)

VENUS RAMIREZ: You mean like this?

STEPHEN ADLY GUIRGIS

(Venus moves closer to her, points out her neck—)

Or like this?
BETTY WOODS: Oh God I'm sorry.

(Venus lifts up her skirt and whips out her dick.)

VENUS RAMIREZ: Or how about his?

(Betty stares at Venus's dick. After a long moment, Venus puts it away.)

What you got down there? There was a time I'd kill to have that. And I felt it from age five.
BETTY WOODS: I'm sorry.
VENUS RAMIREZ: Don't be. I'm not. I didn't grow up with advantages. Or parents who had a fuckin' clue. I mean, don't get me wrong, honey—I woulda preferred a hole to a pole from the get-go, but a cock and balls don't define me, and they don't make me what I'm not. This ain't the body I was supposed to have. But ya gotta work with what you got, sister.
BETTY WOODS: And you do! You're, you're—
VENUS RAMIREZ: I'm beautiful, I know. And girl—it's a blessing and a curse. But I used to hate every inch of me. That's what the society told me to feel about myself. Just like they told you. Well fuck that. And I ain't proud of every aspect of my day to day, I still suck dick and give up ass for cash, I self-medicate a little dope on the once in a while, fell on some hard times, but I love every inch of myself head to toe—lips, hips, fingertips—cuz they don't get to tell me about me, I tell them. And you should too.

(Venus hands Betty the scrub brush.)

You got this from here. Scrub down there. Pussy and ass.
I'm a go smoke.

(Venus goes to exit.)

BETTY WOODS: I don't know how to thank you.
VENUS RAMIREZ: I'll take cash when you got it. In the meantime:
Love Yourself.

SCENE 9

Park Bench Across the Street. Midnight.

Bella sits on bench, smoking, headphones on; Little Freddy sleeps in his carriage. After a moment, Venus enters.

VENUS RAMIREZ: Hey!!!

BELLA: Hey, mama.

VENUS RAMIREZ: Okay—can I just say—I had the most intense evening, it was beautiful and spiritual and empowering and I empowered someone and in turn received empowerment from my empowering—and I was high on self-esteem, and I wore it like a Givenchy wedding gown, but then, I was like, "Ay, all this self-esteem is making me VERY uncomfortable," but I completed my service, and now here I am—and I just wanted to say all that to you—and also— I love your tetas, mami. Can I touch them?

BELLA: Sure.

VENUS RAMIREZ: Wow. Can I—a little squeeze?

BELLA: Knock yourself out.

VENUS RAMIREZ: Can I see them?

BELLA: You can do lines off them—if you're holding.

VENUS RAMIREZ: Oh yes, as promised!

(Venus takes out bags, Bella examines.)

BELLA: Cute stamps. Good stuff?

VENUS RAMIREZ: It's from the Heights, six people OD'd on it over the weekend.

BELLA: Cool . . . Um, I couldn't get money, but—

(Venus starts preparing shots.)

VENUS RAMIREZ: Please! I got you. Sister got a sister. Now how are you?

BELLA: Carmen and I made up.

VENUS RAMIREZ: Oh . . . That's, that's good.

BELLA: It is good. You've only seen one side of her.

VENUS RAMIREZ: I'm not judging, mama. Snorting or booting?

BELLA: Booting. Take my lighter.

VENUS RAMIREZ: Thanks. So, you two made up, and . . . ?

BELLA: What? We had an amazing time, we tore up the sheets.

VENUS RAMIREZ: What about romance?

(A quick beat. Bella sighs.)

BELLA: . . . Yeah, that too . . . Like a lot . . . And she loves Freddy Junior. And look at him—he sleeps now. Ever since I met her, all of the sudden he does everything normal. Like he's happy.

VENUS RAMIREZ: And are you happy?

BELLA: Yeah I'm happy, okay—what are you, fuckin' Oprah?

VENUS RAMIREZ: Sorry.

BELLA: I'm dancing on air—about to throw away thirty-four days clean because I'm so fuckin' happy.

VENUS RAMIREZ: Mama, we don't have to do this—

BELLA: I've been waiting all day to do this—that's my point. Me and Carmen, we make up, we have a great time, she's very—I dunno—she's not full of shit. She's sincere. She disarms me. I can't help it. I forget myself. I tell her things. I feel things. Real things. About her—but also about how maybe it's okay, like I could be redeemable, and I let her love in, because that's what normal people do, right—but the whole time, I'm thinking about meeting you, getting high—and it makes me wanna jump off a fuckin' bridge—

VENUS RAMIREZ: I think you're scared—

BELLA: Stop it. I mean, c'mon. Do you, like, only get high alone? Cuz really, no offense, Venus—but your drug-side manner fuckin' sucks. "Are you happy?" "Is it romance?" "I think you're scared"—who says that shit when you're trying to get high?

VENUS RAMIREZ: I'm sorry.

BELLA: It's okay, just lighten up.

VENUS RAMIREZ: I do get high alone. I don't, I don't have people right now.

BELLA: I'm your people, Venus. Let's just chill. And I'm fine. You know the deal: Half the time ya wanna throw yourself off a bridge, the other half you're like legitimately pissed no one's named a bridge after you.

(She takes a brand-new pint of Jack Daniels out of her baby carriage, opens it, and sips.)

Oh hot damn that's good. Here—have some.

VENUS RAMIREZ: Sure.

(Venus drinks. Bella drinks again.)

BELLA: So fuckin' good, right? And it's never gonna not be good. I don't care what anybody says, like, "Dude, I slipped: I shot ten baggies, drank a case of vodka, snorted Peru— but, ya know—it just didn't work for me, it doesn't work anymore." Bullshit. It works. All of it. Always has, always will. Some things are just good. I hate when people are self-deluded, ya know?

VENUS RAMIREZ: Definitely.

BELLA: You like Tom Petty?

VENUS RAMIREZ: Oh yeah, mami!

BELLA: If I ever went back to dick, it'd be Tom Petty. If, like, he wasn't dead. I never met him, but you could just tell: He gets it.

VENUS RAMIREZ: He does.

BELLA: "Oh my my, oh hell yes," right?

VENUS RAMIREZ: Absolutely! Except—actually, I lied, I don't know who he is! But I want you to like me, because I think we could be really good girlfriends.

BELLA: Sure, me too.

VENUS RAMIREZ: You want me to fix you?

BELLA: Yeah.

VENUS RAMIREZ: Wow, you got great veins!

BELLA: I know.

(Venus shoots her up.)

VENUS RAMIREZ: Okay, mami, one, two . . . .

(Bella receives the hit, sighs. Her face becomes pure pleasure. Venus shoots herself. She immediately begins nodding.)

You . . . gonna be . . . my best friend . . .

BELLA: This is my meditation. So beautiful.

(Venus nods out. Bella stares up at the sky; she is beaming with pleasure.)

"Oh my my." Beautiful. Beautiful . . .

(Bella is gone—but conscious.)

SCENE 10

Community Room. Two A.M.

In darkness, Wanda is alone watching TV with the sound very low. She drinks straight vodka through a straw out of her Ensure carton. She eats a single saltine cracker, breaking it off in tiny pieces. This is her happy place, and here she doesn't look like a dying woman wasting away in a wheelchair—she looks like a bright-eyed child who snuck into the living room after bedtime to watch TV.

Wanda watches, when suddenly, the room lights go on to about half, startling her—

MISS RIVERA: I figured that had to be you.

> (*Rivera has her coat and bag; she's leaving for the night. She drinks a vodka martini out of her Starbucks cup.*)

WANDA WHEELS: Oh my!! Who's that?! Miss Rivera?!

MISS RIVERA: How you doing, Miss Wanda?

WANDA WHEELS: C'mon now. You scared hell out of me—almost gave me my wish!

MISS RIVERA: And what's that?

WANDA WHEELS: Heart attack and die.

MISS RIVERA: Stop.

WANDA WHEELS: What time is it, my dear?

MISS RIVERA: Two A.M.

WANDA WHEELS: Why you still here?

MISS RIVERA: Paperwork, what do you think? No office staff— you know Miss Soto who answers the phones?

WANDA WHEELS: Nice lady.

MISS RIVERA: Lovely woman. But I asked for an administrative assistant, they give me an eighty-year-old Jehovah Witness with cataracts and advanced glaucoma.

WANDA WHEELS: Oh Lord, no—

(Just then, Nicky wanders in drunk.)

NICKY: I'm here to see my fuckin' wife!

(Nicky starts to advance, Rivera pulls mace from her purse, and rushes him.)

MISS RIVERA: Hey! Get outta here! We're closed! Get on out! Go!

NICKY: Hey! Hey! . . . *(As he runs out)* . . . Bitch!

(Nicky exits.)

WANDA WHEELS: Calls you a bitch, but he's the one running.

MISS RIVERA: Three months they been promising a night security guard . . . Anyway, what are you watching there?

(Rivera grabs her drink and crosses to Wanda.)

WANDA WHEELS: Well, since you asked—may I take you into my confidence?

MISS RIVERA: Why? Whatchu got?

WANDA WHEELS: Would you care for a drink, Miss Rivera?

MISS RIVERA: I don't drink, Wanda. Got my coffee right here.

WANDA WHEELS: Umm-hmm. You got your "coffee," I got my "Ensure." I can dance that number. Anyway, this movie here—

MISS RIVERA: Yeah, I don't know it.

WANDA WHEELS: You ain't alone. But you see that handsome double hunk of man cleaning his gun?

MISS RIVERA: He fine.

WANDA WHEELS: Yes he is. And that man—used to be *my* man.

MISS RIVERA: What?

WANDA WHEELS: Sssh. Don't tell nobody.

MISS RIVERA: That man was your man?

WANDA WHEELS: Oh I had several darlin', but he, yeah, I was fond of him.

MISS RIVERA: You lying to me?

WANDA WHEELS: Wait, wait, wait . . . hold on, hold on—okay! You see that pretty dancer girl he's eyeing?

MISS RIVERA: Yeah, so—oh my God! Oh my God!

WANDA WHEELS: Sssh! Sssssh!

MISS RIVERA: That's you!

WANDA WHEELS: In another life, yes . . . I don't need nobody to know. But it's nice that now one person does know . . . Now: How's your daughter?

MISS RIVERA: She's not talking to me. Teenagers, ya know?

WANDA WHEELS: I wouldn't know.

MISS RIVERA: Her father, the philandering deadbeat, he lives in Atlanta, got remarried to an attorney, in your old business, entertainment lawyer, she's got money, so now he's got money, and they take my Isabella on trips, send her gifts . . .

WANDA WHEELS: Well, at least he's meeting his responsibilities.

MISS RIVERA: . . . Last month, when she was there, they looked at high schools, private schools, she told me this tonight on the phone, she wants to go live with them

WANDA WHEELS: Well, that ain't on the table, right?

MISS RIVERA: I don't know. She hates me.

WANDA WHEELS: She wants to spend more time with you.

MISS RIVERA: What time? Look at me. Two A.M., I'm here with you.

WANDA WHEELS: I enjoy our time together. On the late-night witching hour. But this place, it's a refuge, not a destination. This is where you work. Believe me, I did what you do, but I did it in theaters, dance studios, bars, bedrooms, after-hours joints, drug dens, motel rooms and hotel lobbies. The only real destination is home. I never got there. There isn't a woman here who doesn't wish she had a destination. You do. I heard the city offered you a job for more money and less hours. Take it. Shed your refuge. Punch a clock and go home. Home, miss. Home. Click your heels and go.

MISS RIVERA: Uh-huh, sure. Like *The Wizard of Oz*, right?

(Melba enters with Sugar and Rosie, all in pajamas and bath-robes—)

LITTLE MELBA DIAZ: Y'all watching *The Wizard of Oz*?

QUEEN SUGAR: We was hoping whoever down here had some kinda stash of brownies, cakes, or pie.

ROCKAWAY ROSIE: Oh, hello, Miss Rivera—

MISS RIVERA: Hiya, Rosie—

ROCKAWAY ROSIE: Oh oh oh—Miss Rivera—Roberta from the church, you know—with the odd voice, she said to tell you—oh no, what was it? Oh no—no no no no no—

MISS RIVERA: Well, that's my cue! Goodnight, ladies!

ROCKAWAY ROSIE: No no no—no no no—Roberta said, she said—

(Rivera exits.)

Well, okay, I'll, I'll, I'll tell her in the morning, yeah—
QUEEN SUGAR: Whatchu watching, Wanda?
WANDA WHEELS: Oh nothing—
QUEEN SUGAR: Nothing?! He fine!

(Melba rushes to the TV.)

LITTLE MELBA DIAZ: Who fine?!

(Just then the door flies open.)

QUEEN SUGAR: Miss Rivera?

*(Venus staggers in from the doorway, pushing Bella's baby car-
riage. They all stare at her—she notices them, gives them a slow-
motion wave and hello—)*

VENUS RAMIREZ: Oh—heeeeeeey! Whatchu all doing up? I was
just . . . for a walk . . .
LITTLE MELBA DIAZ: Hey—Venus, where's Bella?!
ROCKAWAY ROSIE: Yeah, where's Bella?
WANDA WHEELS: Venus?! Venus?!

*(Venus raises her hand as if to say "one second," she thinks and
thinks and thinks and—remembers—and—bursts into tears—)*

VENUS RAMIREZ: Ay, ay, ay—I don't know! But I didn't do nuthin! I just went for air! I just—

*(The baby starts to cry. The women go attend to it. Venus col-
lapses in a heap in Wanda's arms. Blackout.)*

Act Two

SCENE 1

Building Exterior. The Following Morning.

Joey, over by the curb, is sweeping. Father Miguel sips coffee, trying to read the Daily News. *Mateo sits next to him eating a jelly doughnut, sipping chocolate milk—and talking.*

MATEO: This a good doughnut, Father. You got it from where you live at, right?

FATHER MIGUEL: Yes.

MATEO: In Jersey City, right?

FATHER MIGUEL: Yes.

MATEO: Yeah. I could tell. Things from Jersey be more fresher sometimes.

FATHER MIGUEL: . . . Uh-huh.

MATEO: Yeah . . . Jersey City—that's in New Jersey, right?

FATHER MIGUEL: . . . Uh-huh.

MATEO: Yeah . . . Sometimes I wonder though: If Jersey City's in New Jersey, why don't they just call it New Jersey City? Ya know?

FATHER MIGUEL: Mateo.

MATEO: Nah, cuz, this is New York City, right? We don't call it "York City"—cuz that'd be mad stupid, right?

(Father Miguel sighs, gives up, puts down his paper.)

That's why New York's the best, and Jersey ain't. Hey Father: How did the gorilla get down the stairs? He slid down the banana-ster!

(Wanda, Sugar, Rosie, Betty, Melba, Munchies, Taina, Sonia and Sarge approach the entrance with somber expressions.)

ROCKAWAY ROSIE: Good morning, Father.

QUEEN SUGAR: No luck, Father.

MATEO: Where were y'all at?

LITTLE MELBA DIAZ: Looking for Bella.

(Rivera appears up the block, arriving for work, heading their way.)

Uh-oh—Miss Rivera.

(The women hustle inside. Rivera pauses to check a text on her phone. Sarge remains.)

SARGE: Little Freddy's okay?

FATHER MIGUEL: Yes.

SARGE: Cuz I could take care of him till Bella comes back.

FATHER MIGUEL: It's better this way. If Rivera found out, she'd have to call social services. This way, if Bella comes back—

SARGE: She's coming back!

FATHER MIGUEL: Yes. And when she does, Little Freddy will be waiting.

SARGE: But he's safe?

FATHER MIGUEL: He's with the nuns at Corpus Christi. They can keep a secret. Have I kept my word to you so far?

SARGE: Yeah.

FATHER MIGUEL: Then you keep your word to me.

(Rivera approaches.)

MISS RIVERA: Good morning . . . Sarge, wait, I found a VA on Borden Avenue that has medical and housing—

SARGE: Yeah, yeah, not interested, thanks.

(Sarge exits down the block to continue looking for Bella.)

MISS RIVERA: Something up with Sarge?

FATHER MIGUEL: No. Think she just got up on the wrong side of the bed.

MISS RIVERA: She was born on the wrong side of the bed. And Iraq didn't help. *(To Mateo)* What're you looking at?

MATEO: Nothing.

MISS RIVERA: Get inside. Go. You want socks?

MATEO: Yeah.

MISS RIVERA: Move your ass then.

(Rivera and Mateo exit inside. Father Miguel sits, picks up his paper, starts to open it, when—)

NICKY: Hey Father.

FATHER MIGUEL: Turn around and go. You can't be here.

NICKY: I wanna see my wife.

(Father Miguel rises.)

FATHER MIGUEL: They tell me in Brooklyn you dropped out of the domestic violence program.

NICKY: Yeah, thanks for that. Great neighborhood. They stole my car . . . Frank Thompson. Remember him?

FATHER MIGUEL: . . . Who?

NICKY: I'll give you a hint: He fell off a roof on Avenue B the year the Rangers won the cup. Want another hint?

(Beat.)

FATHER MIGUEL: Are you threatening me?

NICKY: My priest knows you. Says I was right, you're a gay boy. Says you weren't entirely wrong what you did to this Frank Thompson back in the day, but if you don't want trouble for yourself and for this place—you'll let me go upstairs, fix things with my wife.

FATHER MIGUEL: Does he know what you did to her?

NICKY: He believes in the sanctity of marriage.

(Nicky snaps a photo of Father Miguel with his cell phone.)

I wanna see my wife. Right. The. Fuck. Now.

(Beat.)

FATHER MIGUEL: Okay. Follow me. *(Gesturing)* Right this way.

NICKY: Not through the doors there?

FATHER MIGUEL: Back entrance. I could get in a lot of trouble.

NICKY: Yeah yeah don't wet your pants.

FATHER MIGUEL: This way.

(Gestures for Nicky to lead the way.)

NICKY: Turn here?

FATHER MIGUEL: Yeah. But quietly.

(As Nicky turns into the alley, Father Miguel removes his belt, folds it in half to fashion it as a weapon, and follows Nicky down the alley, as—

Mateo, Melba and Taina exit the building and sit on the stoop. Melba smokes. Taina hits her weed vape, takes a deep hit.)

MATEO: You gonna get us all in trouble if they catch you smoking weed out here.

TAINA: I don't give a fuck.

LITTLE MELBA DIAZ: I could get a hit?

(Taina passes it.)

MATEO: You traveling down the wrong path, Taina. You too, Melba.

TAINA: Seriously, Mateo: We liked you bettah when you was bad.

LITTLE MELBA DIAZ: Yeah. Take a hit, Mateo. C'mon, papa.

MATEO: Fuck that. Y'all ain't gonna "crabs in a barrel" me. I got dreams.

TAINA: Wet dreams! Mucho puneta—that's why you bald an' shit!

MATEO: I got hair if I want hair, but I don't want it. And Melba knows what I'm talking about. That's why she a straight-A student—cuz she got dreams too, right, Melba?

LITTLE MELBA DIAZ: Thass true. I'm a join the military or go to college or be a writer like that Betty Woods—you know she's a writer? She showed me online—bitch wrote books!

TAINA: For real?

LITTLE MELBA DIAZ: Yup. Anyway, I'm a do something. I ain't trying to live my whole life here, like some people.

TAINA: . . . Some people like who?!

LITTLE MELBA DIAZ: Nah, nah—I didn't mean you, you my girl, T.

TAINA: I ain't here by choice. I gotta look after my mother.

LITTLE MELBA DIAZ: No doubt, no doubt. And that shit's honorable. Right, Mateo? That shit is lit!

MATEO: It ain't lit—it's un lit. It's fuckin', you like a soggy pack of wet matches, Taina.

TAINA: You corny—corny for real.

MATEO: You could deny it, but you and me, we gotta lot in common. 'Cept I'm a minor, so I gotta be here. But you, I mean you fine and all—but peep the mirror, boo—you ain't no minor, you—old.

TAINA: I ain't old!

LITTLE MELBA DIAZ: You kinda old, mama, but you fly as fuck! Ain't she fly, Mateo?

MATEO: I wish she would fly.

TAINA: Meaning what?

MATEO: Meaning you know what the fuck I mean. You depressing. All you do is smoke weed and complain about your moms. I used to wanna get with you. Now you just sad an' shit. An' old.

(From Mobo's window upstairs, Sonia sticks her head out.)

HAPPY MEAL SONIA: Taina! I need you up here!

TAINA: Coming, Ma.

(Mobo sticks his head out, sees them all smoking.)

MR. MOBO: No smoking, no loitering! The neighbors will complain, I'm serious!

(Mobo pops back inside. Sugar and Munchies enter and hit the stoop.)

QUEEN SUGAR: Who smokin' weed out here?!

(Sugar snatches the weed—and starts smoking it.)

MATEO: Right Taina's old, Miss Sugar?

QUEEN SUGAR: She ain't old.

MATEO: . . . But she depressing as fuck though, right?

QUEEN SUGAR: Oh. Very . . . It's true, girl. And we all like you, but every time someone try to hang with you, they gotta hang with "Cuckoo for Cocoa Puffs" too. This some good-ass reefer, though!

(Mobo bursts through the doors.)

MR. MOBO: No loitering. No smoking. No marijuana. Melba, Mateo—inside! Taina, go to your mother! Sugar—

(Melba, Mateo and Taina exit.)

QUEEN SUGAR: Hey Mister Mobo! I got those Fam-Way papers for you to sign—I just need your deposit, and then, just watch, couple months—you gonna be King of Nigeria for real!

MR. MOBO: . . . Sugar—

QUEEN SUGAR: There's not a problem is there?

MR. MOBO: No. Just. Well. Financially, um, well—I'm afraid I must reconsider—

QUEEN SUGAR: But you're still considering?

MR. MOBO: No.

(Sugar turns immediately and irately to Munchies.)

QUEEN SUGAR: You told him—didn't you?!

MUNCHIES: I didn't tell him! Wanda told him!

QUEEN SUGAR: Wanda??!!

MR. MOBO: Yes, Wanda mentioned—

QUEEN SUGAR: Wanda?! Wanda?!

(Sugar becomes emotional, rushes inside. Munchies and Mobo are alone. Munchies goes in for some tongue—)

MR. MOBO: No, no. Please! It is not proper.

MUNCHIES: Okay. I get it. I can do down low.

MR. MOBO: No. No down low. What we did last night—

MUNCHIES: And the night before that, and the night before that—

MR. MOBO: Yes. Yes. I know.

MUNCHIES: That shit was, like—"Blam!" "Blam blam!" "Blam blam tsunami blam blam!"

MR. MOBO: Tsunami, yes. But no more.

MUNCHIES: Whatchu mean?

MR. MOBO: I mean no more.

MUNCHIES: But Mobo—

MR. MOBO: No. No. It cannot be. We are concluded.

MUNCHIES: Concluded? You like some other bitch don't you?

MR. MOBO: No. No. Maybe. I am having a coffee date with Jennifer.

MUNCHIES: Nigga—what? Jennifer from here?! The counselor?

MR. MOBO: It's just social. Getting to know you. It is not improper. But you and me—improper!

MUNCHIES: Oh you bitch-ass, no-account, sistuh-hating, African Wonder Bread Poindexter sunovabitch!

MR. MOBO: Collect yourself! Collect yourself to respect yourself! I am sorry! You are fire! But I cannot! It cannot be! I go now!

(Mobo ducks back inside. Munchies seethes, tries to kick something, and finally breaks down—sobs.)

SCENE 2

Group Therapy in the Community Room. Early Evening.

In the room, Rosie, Sarge, Jennifer, Wanda, Betty, Melba, Taina and Sonia. At a bit of a distance from them, Joey mops the floor.

ROCKAWAY ROSIE: No no no no! Sarge, I wasn't—what's the expression—oh, yeah, yeah, yeah, yeah! "Dissing"! No no no no no, I wasn't dissing—

SARGE: Good cuz I expect more from you!

ROCKAWAY ROSIE: More, yes! Way more! Much more! And no dissing. No no no no no.

SARGE: Cuz it sounded like you was dissing and I don't abide no sideways snakes!!

JENNIFER: I think Rosie has made clear—

ROCKAWAY ROSIE: Oh no—very clear, the clearest! And snakes??! Heebie-jeebies! Snaky, slithering, maneuvering—oh no! Oh no no no no no!

(Munchies enters.)

JENNIFER: You're late—
MUNCHIES: Sorry, miss—you know I ain't usually tardy—
JENNIFER: That's true—take a seat.
MUNCHIES *(Sitting)*: Yeah, on days when a home-wrecking ho don't steal my man—I'm punctual like a motherfucker!
JENNIFER: Excuse me?

(Munchies notices Joey staring at her.)

MUNCHIES: Who you lookin' at? Mop the floor, bitch!
JENNIFER: Sit down, Munchies!
MUNCHIES: Or what?
SARGE: Munchies—sit the fuck down!

(Munchies complies.)

JENNIFER: Okay then. Now: Rosie—you were saying?? Please continue.
ROCKAWAY ROSIE: Continue. Yes . . . No. Just—what you said, Sarge, about "you know who," about Bella—um—
SARGE: Yeah yeah. I don't wanna talk about it. And she ain't even, we ain't married, she ain't my whatever, I ain't her fiancée—
ROCKAWAY ROSIE: Fiancée! Fiancée! Yes! I remember now. I was gonna say, about your "you know who," I'm so sorry, Sarge, in particular because—okay, look I was raised not to put your dirty undies, your brassiere and hose, you don't put them in the corner laundromat, you wash them in the sink when the men have gone to bed—you know, in private, but I love you, Sarge, so—aw the hell with it—I know how you feel!
SARGE: C'mon, Ro—I don't feel nuthin!

ROCKAWAY ROSIE: No no no no no, you feel! You feel, Sarge. You're a good girl. I know. You act tough, with the you know, oh you know—bravado and (you didn't hear this, Jennifer)—fisticuffs, and the foul, foul language—but I know you. Your heart. You're like my Aunt Bess. Oh poor Aunt Bess . . .

SARGE: I ain't no Aunt Bess—

JENNIFER: Is that what you wanted to share?

ROCKAWAY ROSIE: Yeah yeah yeah yeah yeah yeah—oh! No no no no—I know your pain, Sarge—I wanted to share—I had a fiancé once. Sarge—my fiancé, I had a fiancé, Sarge, a smooth talker, bedroom eyes, slim-hipped, smirky dimples—he looked like, well, he looked just like Mickey Rourke, okay, but the younger, normal-ish Mickey—you know—Poor Irish Trash But Redeemable, rascally—oh he had me over the moon! He took me to the movies, oh, he had me—no one ever made me feel special—and he made me feel so, I can't even say—but in the movie theater, when he, you know, he touched my breasts—and my eyes went cross-eyed I couldn't even see the screen!

(Suddenly an outburst from Munchies who has been eyeballing Joey, muttering to herself and nodding disapprovingly—)

MUNCHIES: That ain't how you do it!!!! Miss: Look at that bald-headed, no-account, job-corp, Special Olympic "Retardo Montalbán" thug-ass nigga over there! He thinking he mopping shit, he just moving dirt around!

ROCKAWAY ROSIE: The night he proposed, I gave myself to him, you know, all the way? And with his you know, those slim hips and smooth talking smooth talk, tossled hair, and afterwards, oh you could have melted me with butter, and then he got dressed, told me he was going down the corner for some smokes and a couple of hot-crossed buns, it was close to Easter, you know, Lent?

MUNCHIES: Hey! Mr. Potato Head! You just stirring up germs, bacterias, filth and spores up into the air! That ain't mopping! That ain't how you fuckin' do it!

JENNIFER: Munchies, please!

MUNCHIES: Please what? Contract fuckin' Ebola behind this clown-head clown's spread of infectious organisms an' shit?! I'm supposed to die cuz of this minimum-wage Ronald McDonald House special-ed nigga?

ROCKAWAY ROSIE: He never came back, my fiancé, went into the wind, I thought maybe I don't know, he got scared—but in the morning, underneath my sink, my life savings—in a box of Tide laundry detergent, he took it, he took it all—

MUNCHIES: Yo! You see what he doing? He ain't even rinse the mop!

ROCKAWAY ROSIE: Three months later he married a whore from the Key Food, they moved in right down my block, I never said a word, my life savings and all, but I was mortified—

MUNCHIES: Yo. Put that mop down, bitch!

ROCKAWAY ROSIE: He broke my heart, I was never the same again—

BETTY WOODS: I feel you, Rosie.

SARGE: What?

BETTY WOODS: I said I feel Rosie. I feel you too, Sarge. Obviously you've had a lot on your mind. I harbor no ill will, okay? No hard feelings?

SARGE: . . . Yeah. Yeah, okay, Betty. And uh Rosie, I feel you too.

LITTLE MELBA DIAZ: Me too.

TAINA: Me too.   HAPPY MEAL SONIA: Me too.

ROCKAWAY ROSIE: Aw, he was a bum, I had a thing for bums—but you know, Sarge, when you got that feeling for someone, I mean, the sun rose and set on that man, and for a few months I was walking three feet off the ground, and I was in LOVE, and soda pop tasted like champagne and it was effortless to be nice, and I was so alive I'd shiver joy and well-being even in ninety-eight-degree humidity! And I just hope that, "you know who," because, there's nothing worse than a broken heart, Sarge—it's thirty years later and you can still stick a fork in me, and I don't want that for YOU!

(Rosie starts to cry. Wanda wheels over to comfort her. Munchies rises, makes a beeline for Joey, and takes the mop out of his hand.)

JENNIFER: Uh, Munchies! Munchies, I don't think that's—

MUNCHIES: First of all, you don't supposed to mop up and down, you gotta do it side to side!

JOEY FRESCO: I know that!

MUNCHIES: Then why you do it wrong for?! And you gotta clean the water, bitch!

JOEY FRESCO: Don't call me that!

MUNCHIES: I'll call you what the fuck I want, bitch-ass bald-headed bitch! You ain't no real janitor! And you ain't know the first thing about sanitationalism! You a minimum-wage, rent-a-retard, jailhouse-bottom bitch!

JOEY FRESCO: Don't say that!

MUNCHIES: Or what?!

JOEY FRESCO: You don't say that! I don't have to take none of that.

MUNCHIES: You take whatever the fuck I dish out, and damn—is that your breath?! Damn, you got filth in your mouth! Crest, nigga—Crest! *(To Jennifer)* Yo! How he allowed to work here with this hazardous-waste breath and mopping like— *(To Joey)* What you got something to say?!

JOEY FRESCO: This ain't right! You, you, you, you ain't right!

MUNCHIES: Eyeball me one more time I'll make a potato head nigga blind!

JENNIFER: Sarge—can you help here?

SARGE: Why?

(Joey, in a fury, tears now streaming down his face, runs to the corner, turns to Munchies—)

JOEY FRESCO: I'm on parole! And you ain't right.

(Joey starts doing rapid-fire push-ups to calm his fury. He does not stop.)

JENNIFER: Munchies! You need to leave!

MUNCHIES: Oh I most definitely need to leave! But just remember this, ya Mayberry bitch: I'm a Baby Back Bouncing Juicy Prime Rib Full Grown Delicious Sister Queen, okay? And X-rated! And once a man had all that—and he DID—then y'all two could go to all the museums you want, drink tea, adopt a puppy, get married by the Queen of England, it don't matter—he ain't never gonna have no actual lust in his loin for some Mild Honey Barbeque Arby's Chicken Wing like you!

(Munchies goes to exit and bumps into Venus, who is entering. Munchies addresses Venus:)

And fuck you too!

(Munchies exits.)

JENNIFER: Can someone tell me what that was all about?

(Venus sits.)

SARGE *(To Venus)*: Are you fuckin' serious?! Nobody wants you here! And you only alive right now cuz I haven't killed you yet!

(Sarge rises, an empty half-pint liquor bottle falls out from her things. Everybody notices.)

JENNIFER: Okay, Sarge—please sit.

SARGE: Nah!

JENNIFER: Mister Fresco! Mister Fresco! Can you help here, please?

VENUS RAMIREZ: I didn't do nothing wrong, Sarge. I rescued the baby! I came back!

SARGE: You're a fucking liar!

(Joey crosses—)

JOEY FRESCO: Okay, ladies—that ain't for here, this ain't for everybody's ears—

SARGE: I see right through you! I see you! And if she don't come back, if anything happened to her—I don't care who hears it—Jennifer, here—your janitor Romeo over there—I'm gonna kill you! Know that shit! Cuz I will!

VENUS RAMIREZ: You're upset, you're drunk—I don't judge, I empathize—

SARGE: Fuck your empathy. Fuck your fake sympathy act, trying to cover your tracks—

VENUS RAMIREZ: Okay, I understand why you would feel that way—

SARGE: Don't tell me how I feel! Who the fuck are you to know how the fuck I feel??!! Just know—it's coming. Even if she's just fine. You're dead! And I can't wait!

VENUS RAMIREZ: You don't know me.

SARGE: Get out my face, mister.

VENUS RAMIREZ: I'm a woman—but more than that, my core identity, from birth, conditioning, serial abuse and abandonment, being defiled and debased—set on fire—by

family members—force-fed rat poison—and hey, I'm sure
you got your horror stories too, mama—but the result of
all that, Sarge—push me too far, I fight back, I fight dirty,
and I don't know from stopping, bitch—so—one woman to
the other: A bitch been warned!!

(Blackout.)

SCENE 3

Out Front and Upstairs. That Night.

Wanda smokes, squinting and straining her eyes to keep reading her old, worn-out copy of Langston Hughes's The Weary Blues.

   Joey jogs over to her, hands her a half-pint bottle in a brown paper bag and her change—

JOEY FRESCO: Here ya go, Miss Wanda, and here's your change and receipt.

WANDA WHEELS: Keep the change, baby.

JOEY FRESCO: No, Miss Wanda. Just—the bottle ain't come from me, okay, and you got some matches?

   (Wanda hands him a lighter.)

WANDA WHEELS: Keep it. And these.

(She hands him several Hershey bars.)

JOEY FRESCO: No, no—you need to eat those for your calories—
WANDA WHEELS: Don't want 'em.
JOEY FRESCO: Okay, but, I don't eat that, I got allergies, so—
WANDA WHEELS: For your kids then.

(He doesn't take them from her.)

You did time, right? So you know what it's like to have others make decisions for you. I can feed myself—by myself—as it pleases myself. Or not. Now, you're a good man, so let's leave it at that.
JOEY FRESCO: Okay. Yes, ma'am.

(Joey pockets the candy, dashes over to the alley, where Venus is. He leans against the building and lights a forlorn Venus's cigarette. She takes a drag, passes it to him, rests her head on his shoulder.
Wanda pours vodka into her empty Ensure carton, sips through a straw, resumes reading.
Sugar, in a robe and slippers, exits the building in a huff.)

WANDA WHEELS: Oh hey there, Queenie—up late too, huh? How are ya, sister?
QUEEN SUGAR: I ain't conversating with you, I'm only here for the air!
WANDA WHEELS: . . . Okay.
QUEEN SUGAR: Yeah. So don't be "Hey Queenie-ing" me, or calling me Sister or Homegirl or Boogie Down or Big Foot or Sweet Potato or any of that—like we familiar or something.
WANDA WHEELS: . . . Okay.
QUEEN SUGAR: Cuz we ain't.
WANDA WHEELS: Okay.
QUEEN SUGAR: Not no more, Slim!

WANDA WHEELS: Sorry to hear that.

QUEEN SUGAR: You should be. No more of me hanging on your every word like a fool, you frontin' like you was droppin' science—trying to be all wise like you was Yoda or some shit. Anyway, we done. And I'll be leaving here soon anyway—despite your attempts at economic sabotage—because I believe in myself, ya hear? Don't answer, can't hear ya, we done.

WANDA WHEELS: Well . . . It's a free country—at least that's what they would have you believe . . .

(Beat. Wanda becomes lost in thought.)

Free country. Yeah . . . I remember it was Noam Chomsky who helped dispel me of that myth—one night at the Café Carlyle where he took me for a drink—that was almost thirty years ago, 1990 I believe . . . And I should've gone home with Amiri Baraka that night. He liked a girl on his arm from time to time for reasons that don't bear repeating and he was fond of me. Brilliant man. Vicious. Wounded. Brilliant. Just brilliant. Anyway, I was a chorus girl on Broadway at the time—and Noam—Noam Chomsky—he was friends with my poetry professor, who I was dating, and he took Noam to my show, but he had to leave right after, so Noam, he offered to take me for a drink—it wasn't amorous or nothing—at least not at first—he was pleasant looking but plain—but my God, his brain! And his politics! Not to mention—

QUEEN SUGAR: Excuse me—did you not hear me say I ain't interested in conversating and that we done?!

WANDA WHEELS: Of course I heard you—

QUEEN SUGAR: Then why you still yacking?!

WANDA WHEELS: I'm sorry. I thought we were just passing the time—and I know you like my stories, and now, Noam Chomsky—

QUEEN SUGAR: Fuck Noam Chomsky! The days of me hanging on your every word—like you was some kinda knowledgable-type bitch who knows shit—them days is gone! You're a drunk. And a anorexic bag of bones. Faking that wheelchair for a disability check. And you screwed me big time! You told Mobo don't sign up for Fam-Way!

WANDA WHEELS: I only said I thought perhaps it wasn't in his best interest.

QUEEN SUGAR: What about MY best interest?! I'm supposed to be your closest friend—and you don't even like Mobo—

WANDA WHEELS: That's not true—

QUEEN SUGAR: Oh, c'mon, Wanda!

WANDA WHEELS: Mobo annoys me, yes—but only because he's such a Goody Two–Shoes, so anal-retentive about every little rule and regulation, and he's just so damn "Nigerian" about everything—I told you about my first fiancé, the exchange student—but the point of it is, all I really did—

QUEEN SUGAR: YOU TOLD HIM NOT TO INVEST IN FAM-WAY!

WANDA WHEELS: Well, because it's a scam!

QUEEN SUGAR: It's NOT a scam!

WANDA WHEELS: It's a scam, and I do have issues with Mobo, but the poor guy—he doesn't have much money and, Queenie, I mean—he's an immigrant!

QUEEN SUGAR: I needed that sale. I was desperate. And I sold him! I sold that Mobo motherfucker! I'm an ex-con on parole. There's not a lot of chances to make real money for someone like me. And now Fam-Way dumped me and I'm out two hundred dollars—you know how much two hundred dollars is???!!!

WANDA WHEELS: I know, I know—look!

(Wanda takes out her purse. Pulls out maybe one hundred dollars.)

I want to buy Fam-Way. I'll invest. Here. Take it. And I'll show you something else—something I been waiting to ask you a favor on—

QUEEN SUGAR: Favor?!

(Wanda hands Sugar some papers.)

WANDA WHEELS: Insurance papers. Life insurance. Mine. Look on page three. The beneficiary. Look.

QUEEN SUGAR: "Ms. Minerva Jackson"—how you know my government name?!

WANDA WHEELS: Rivera told me. You see that's ten thousand dollars, right?

QUEEN SUGAR: I don't need your money.

WANDA WHEELS: You do . . . And I need your help.

QUEEN SUGAR: With what?

WANDA WHEELS: . . . You know this book? Langston Hughes? "I got the Weary Blues / And I can't be satisfied. / Got the Weary Blues / And can't be satisfied— / I ain't happy no mo' / And I wish that I had died."

(Sugar notices something crazy up the block, waves Wanda off—)

QUEEN SUGAR: What the?! Hold that thought, Wanda!

(Just then, Sonia walks up the block with a goat on a leash. She is very calm and focused, eyes straight ahead, no attempt to conceal the goat—in fact, she walks the goat as if everybody walks goats in the city, no big deal.
As Sonia is passing the alley—)

VENUS RAMIREZ: . . . Did Sonia get a dog?

JOEY FRESCO: Baby that ain't no dog!

(Sonia goes to enter building with the goat—)

WANDA WHEELS: . . . Uh, good evening, Sonia—who's your friend?

HAPPY MEAL SONIA: Oh, hi Wanda.

QUEEN SUGAR: Is that a goat?!

HAPPY MEAL SONIA: No.

(Sonia enters the building. Joey pops out from the alley and calls out to Wanda and Sugar.)

JOEY FRESCO: Excuse me, ladies—but did you just see a—

QUEEN SUGAR: Yes! Bitch had a *goat!* *(To Wanda)* Fuck she doing with a goat?!

WANDA WHEELS: I haven't a clue, dear. And I fear she doesn't either. Now if that had been my Uncle Linford—he woulda sautéed the little fella into a fine curry—but that poor woman, Sugar—I remember her when she was basically right-minded, so, if that goat brings her even a moment's comfort, then hey, "Whatever gets you through the night," I'm all for it.

(Sonia is now entering the room she shares with Taina—who is sound asleep. Sonia jostles her.)

HAPPY MEAL SONIA: Taina, wake up! Wake up, baby! Taina! Taina!

TAINA: Wha?! Wha?! Ma?! What the fuck?! What time is it?

HAPPY MEAL SONIA: It's very late. Close your eyes. I got a gift for you.

TAINA: A gift? Ma, I'm sleeping. Can I get the gift tomorrow?

HAPPY MEAL SONIA: No! Just wake up! Now, hold on—

(Sonia exits, then—)

You ready?

TAINA: Fuck. Yeah, Ma. Ready.

HAPPY MEAL SONIA: Close your eyes.

TAINA: Ma—if I close my eyes they ain't opening again!

HAPPY MEAL SONIA: Just close them!

(Taina complies.)

Okay: one, two, three, and—

(Sonia enters with the goat.)

Surprise!

TAINA: Ma?! What the fuck?!

HAPPY MEAL SONIA: Isn't he cute?

TAINA: Ma. That's a goat. There's a live goat in here!

HAPPY MEAL SONIA: And he's all yours!

TAINA: Mine?! Ma—where'd you get him?

HAPPY MEAL SONIA: Uptown. Riverside Park.

TAINA: Riverside! Oh my God you stole this fuckin' goat, didn't you?!

HAPPY MEAL SONIA: No, I just found him! We found each other. And I know how you love animals.

TAINA: Ma, this is no good! This is fuckin' trouble! We gotta bring him back! Right now!

(Taina tries to take the leash from Sonia.)

HAPPY MEAL SONIA: No! No! No!!

(They struggle for the leash—Sonia bites Taina's hand to release her from the leash—)

TAINA: Aaaah! Aaaah!

(Leash drops to the floor. The goat runs out of the room.)

HAPPY MEAL SONIA: Where'd he go?! Where is he?!

(Sonia tries to leave to find the goat, but Taina slams the door, locks it, shuts off all the lights. In darkness:)

TAINA: Get in bed, Ma! Now! This never happened, okay?! Someone will find him—

(We hear two women scream! Then a third!)

And when they do—we don't know nothing about it! We were asleep at eleven—okay?!

(Another scream and the sound of something crashing to the floor, then the sound of glass breaking! And another scream!)

No matter what happens—deny, deny, deny! Okay, Ma?!

(Now we hear Sarge screaming:)

SARGE *(Offstage)*: What the fuck?! Ya-llah!! Ya-llah!! Ista-SALEEM! SALEEM-NEFSIK!
LITTLE MELBA DIAZ *(Offstage)*: Oh my God, Sarge— No!!!
SARGE *(Offstage)*: Ah-gaf! Af-gaf! In-HANEE! In-HANEE!
ROCKAWAY ROSIE *(Offstage)*: No Sarge—no!!!!
SARGE *(Offstage)*: IR-fa' yed-ay-yick! IRMI-SILAHEK!
LITTLE MELBA DIAZ *(Offstage)*: It's a goat, Sarge—it's just a goat!
SARGE *(Offstage)*: Ya-lla! Ya-llah! Ya-llah!

(We hear Sarge grunt three times from the exertion of inflicting three stab wounds along with the bloodcurdling scream—of a goat.
Sonia is upset.)

HAPPY MEAL SONIA: Mister Skittles?????

(In bed, in darkness, Taina holds her mother tight.)

TAINA: Nothing happened, Ma. Nothing. Deny, deny, deny.

(At the front entrance, Sarge exits the building covered in blood, a knife in her hand. Wanda and Sugar are shocked. Sarge staggers up the block. Rosie, in pajamas, exits the building in a panic—)

ROCKAWAY ROSIE: Sarge! Sarge!

(But Sarge is gone.)

SCENE 4

Park Bench Across the Street. A Few Days Later. Day.

Joey hands Father Miguel a manila envelope. Mateo sits on the bench eating an ice-cream cone.

FATHER MIGUEL: Thanks for this, Joey.

JOEY FRESCO: No problema, Padre. My brother-in-law, he said, "Anything for a man of the cloth." Especially, he said, "A man of the cloth from the hood." He also said keep that envelope in a safe place.

MATEO: What is it?

FATHER MIGUEL: Nothing, Mateo.

MATEO: It's not nothing, Father. It's an envelope.

JOEY FRESCO: You got a problem with your hearing, little man? If Father Mikey says it's nothing—¿¡por que no te callas la fuckin' boca, mamabicho?!

MATEO: I ain't scared of you! You wanna throw down?

FATHER MIGUEL: Leave us, Mateo.

MATEO: But, Father—

FATHER MIGUEL: I'm okay. Everything is okay. Just go.

(As Mateo exits reluctantly—)

MATEO *(To Joey)*: I know about the goat.

(Mateo exits.)

JOEY FRESCO: I'm sorry, Father. You really helped that kid a lot, and he's a good kid, pero avece un pendejito.

FATHER MIGUEL: He's protective of me. And he has the zeal of the newly converted. Like San Pablo de Tarsu. And like they say, "No Saint without a past, no sinner without a future."

JOEY FRESCO: They say that?

FATHER MIGUEL: They do.

JOEY FRESCO: Good to know. Anyway, my brother-in-law, the cop, he said you good to go. The wife beater, his priest, it's taken care of, no one gonna mess with you.

FATHER MIGUEL: Thank you. Uh, I have no money to pay him— or you—

JOEY FRESCO: Wha? No! Nobody want no money, Father. What I need though, if you don't mind, is advice, but like, don't tell nobody—

FATHER MIGUEL: Have I ever?

JOEY FRESCO: That's true. Okay . . . Damn, Father, this is a big one . . . Okay, so, you know I done some bad things. Like a lot of bad things—

FATHER MIGUEL: And you've served your time, and you're making amends.

JOEY FRESCO: Amends, yeah . . . But this is like, I don't think there's any amends for this, Father.

FATHER MIGUEL: You're a good man, Joey. You've been working hard to change—

JOEY FRESCO: Little by little. No doubt. But here's the thing: You know I got a wife, and you know, like, some girls on the side—and I'm working on that, you know, I'm trying to reduce it down to just my wife, but these girls, Father, I mean, they don't go away easy, I don't know what it is about me, but, I'm all man, you know, like old-school— and the ladies, they desire that—that manly manhood got—and they don't wanna part with it, but I'm trying, and I know it's a sin, and I'm working on it, I really am, especially for the sake of my children, Father—which is why I need to talk to you, it's about my children—

FATHER MIGUEL: Are they okay?

JOEY FRESCO: Father, I'm in love. I tried to not be, but I am. I'm in love. And she's got a dick . . . Or, he does . . . Or, like—does God make mistakes like that? Because this guy, he swears he's a fuckin' woman, and he looks like a woman, and he's tender like a woman, and loving and sweet-natured like a woman, and everything he does is exactly like how a woman does—including breaking my fuckin' balls—but the thing is, Father, despite all his womanly virtues, which are plentiful an' shit—he don't got no tetas or the va-jay-jay—and that ain't so bad, but he smell like a dude some-time—and if that ain't enough—homegirl got a dick! I'm going to hell for this, right?

FATHER MIGUEL: No.

JOEY FRESCO: But he got a dick.

FATHER MIGUEL: Does that bother you?

JOEY FRESCO: Not really, but I mean, a dick—that ain't good, right?

FATHER MIGUEL: Joey. Take a breath. Tell me how I can help you.

JOEY FRESCO: . . . Okay . . . I wanna know if she's a woman. And also if God thinks she's a woman. And if she is a woman, then what happened? And also, even if she ain't a woman, I love her, Father. Like for real. Like, I'm like, "Oh. She got my whole heart." Like—and I don't take this light—I wanna leave my wife and be with her. Or him. Or, well you know. But I don't wanna break God's covenant an' shit.

FATHER MIGUEL: God doesn't care who you love. He cares *that* you love. And if Venus says she's a woman—then she's a woman.

JOEY FRESCO: How you know I'm talkin' 'bout Venus?

FATHER MIGUEL: The problem, Joey, is you're married.

JOEY FRESCO: I'll get a divorce.

FATHER MIGUEL: What about your kids?

JOEY FRESCO: Divorce is common, Father. And if God don't mind the dick, I don't think he gonna—

FATHER MIGUEL: Joey. A man takes responsibility. A man doesn't run away from his responsibilities. You made a vow before God—

JOEY FRESCO: I know, but—

FATHER MIGUEL: If you didn't love her, you shouldn't have married her. But you did. And you have young children. There's nothing to discuss. You have feelings for Venus, but it's infatuation—

JOEY FRESCO: No! No—I swear!

FATHER MIGUEL: Your wife needs you. Your children need you. You're being selfish. A man stands up when it's hard. Not just when it's easy. You want to live right, then live right. But if you want permission to leave your wife—you won't get it from me. A man bears sorrow for the love of his children. And his wife. You have a wife. And it doesn't matter what God thinks is right. He wants you to live according to what YOU think is right.

JOEY FRESCO: I don't understand how you could be so liberal about the dick—but so conservative—

FATHER MIGUEL: It's not conservative. You asked my advice. You don't have to take it. You have to ask YOURSELF what's right. And then act on it. That's a man. Action. Don't think the right thing. Do it. You are your own judge. Not God.

JOEY FRESCO: Okay, but apparently, Father, you threw some dude off a roof—and you're telling me *I* gotta do the right thing? My brother-in-law said it was a long time ago, and that the dude, he was a very, very bad dude, but still, you just said, "No Sinner without a future"—

FATHER MIGUEL: You're right. But it's your future I'm concerned about. And Mateo's. And Taina's and Melba's. And all the women. Not that guy's. And not my own. I trust your heart, Joey. You should trust it too.

SCENE 5

Hellos and Goodbyes. Building Entrance. Night.

Sarge sits on steps in front of the building drinking from a half-pint bottle of vodka. She is stone-faced with a thousand-yard stare. Wanda is in her chair reading and sipping vodka from her Ensure carton. Nicky is hidden but lurking in the alley. Betty and Rosie approach the entrance of the building.

When Rosie sees Sarge, she becomes uncomfortable, whispers something to Betty. As they approach the entrance:

BETTY WOODS: Hi Wanda, you coming to my reading?

ROCKAWAY ROSIE: We're doing it in group today. Instead of talk therapy, Jennifer said. Anyway, it's a change of pace.

WANDA WHEELS: I didn't know you were a writer.

BETTY WOODS: Self-published. But I have—well—had—a fairly competitive ranking on Amazon at one time, I mean, for self-published—and in my genre.

WANDA WHEELS: What's your genre?
BETTY WOODS: Um, it's a niche genre?
ROCKAWAY ROSIE: C'mon, Betty.

(They turn away, go to enter—Betty makes a move toward Sarge—Rosie shakes her head no, indicates with her eyes the bottle in Sarge's hand. They walk past Sarge and enter the building. Sarge and Wanda drink in silence.)

WANDA WHEELS: Well . . . Intriguing.

(No reaction from Sarge. Wanda regards Sarge, who is staring into space and drinking. Wanda fishes through her purse, pulls out an old paper coffee cup—)

Sarge. Maybe put it in a paper cup? I got mine right here.

SARGE *(Grabs her crotch)*: Yeah and I got mines right here. Go fuck yourself, Wanda. You ain't never gave me the time of day, looking down on me from your Black Ivory Tower—now you wanna be helpful? Just ignore me—like how all the rest of them fake-ass bitches are doing me now.

(Sarge drinks. Mobo pops his head out of the front door.)

MR. MOBO: Group is starting!

(He closes door, then pops right back.)

And no smoking!!
SARGE: Ain't no one smoking here, Mobo!!

(Mobo studies her, then steps outside.)

MR. MOBO: No—just drinking an open container! C'mon now! If the neighbors see you drinking, it will cause big trouble!

SARGE: Fuck the neighbors!

MR. MOBO: You may not care about this place, Sarge—but I do! Now surrender that bottle! Tout suite! *(To Wanda)* And you—finish your shake!

WANDA WHEELS: You got it, Mobo.

(Wanda sips her drink happily. Sarge looks at Mobo, downs what's left in her bottle and then hands it to him. Mobo shakes his head in disgust.)

MR. MOBO: You know Sarge, I talk to my mother about you when I call home—I do not talk about *you*, Miss Wanda, but I should—because you are very bad also . . . My mother, Sarge—she says some people cannot be helped, they don't want help, and it is very sad, but we are better served to leave them to their fate. Now, I am praying very hard for Bella, okay—

SARGE: —And I appreciate that—

MR. MOBO: Yes—but when I pray for you, I get no answer from God, only that you are too proud for your own good!

SARGE: What the fuck's wrong with that?! I ain't no beggar and I ain't no victim! No one never raised me to have no pride or self-worth—I taught myself that! I carry myself like that! And I ain't changing shit for nobody! Tell God bring Bella back! Tell God bring her back, I'll get on my knees, lick the sidewalk, eat dirt, whatever the fuck He want! Otherwise—fuck Him and fuck your mother too!

MR. MOBO: You have to come down off your throne, Sarge— or some day—you will have no one! Miss Wanda—am I taking you to group, or not?!

(Wanda is shaken by Mobo's forcefulness and also with sadness for Sarge.)

STEPHEN ADLY GUIRGIS

WANDA WHEELS: Yes, please.

(Mobo begins to wheel her to the entrance and up the steps. As he does, he sings Blind Faith's "Can't Find My Way Home," with a residual anger—

As they exit, we still hear Mobo singing, as lights shift to Taina in her room, packing. She is very sad. Her mother, Sonia, enters.)

HAPPY MEAL SONIA: Taina! Taina, guess what?

TAINA: What, Ma?

HAPPY MEAL SONIA: The man downstairs, the nice man who makes eyes at me, he saved a couple of extra pork chops from dinner and he gave it to me in this bag, see?

TAINA: Dass really nice, Ma.

HAPPY MEAL SONIA: He likes my booty!

TAINA: You got a nice booty, Ma.

HAPPY MEAL SONIA: Oh yeah: I told him you bettah put one extra pork chop in there for my baby girl. Otherwise—forget it! Hey: Why's my suitcase on the bed for? Are they messing with our stuff again?

TAINA: No, Ma.

HAPPY MEAL SONIA: Then why?

TAINA: Put on your sweater, Ma.

HAPPY MEAL SONIA: For what?

TAINA: Just put it on.

(Sonia puts on her sweater. Taina picks up the suitcase. Sonia sees this.)

Let's go downstairs, Ma.

HAPPY MEAL SONIA: But I wanna play cards with Rosie. You, me, and Rosie.

TAINA: Not tonight, Ma. We can't.

HAPPY MEAL SONIA: Why not?

TAINA: Because we can't.

HAPPY MEAL SONIA: Because why?

TAINA: . . . Because—there's an Access-A-Ride Van coming.

HAPPY MEAL SONIA: Coming for what?

TAINA: To take you to the hospital.

HAPPY MEAL SONIA: But I don't wanna go to the hospital.

TAINA: I know, but—

HAPPY MEAL SONIA: Plus—you hate it at the hospital.

TAINA: I know, but, I'm not going.

HAPPY MEAL SONIA: You're not?!

TAINA: Just you.

HAPPY MEAL SONIA: Just me? Why just me? Not you and me? Just me?

TAINA: For now.

HAPPY MEAL SONIA: But we don't do that.

TAINA: I know.

HAPPY MEAL SONIA: But I don't wanna go to no hospital!

TAINA: I know, Ma. But you gotta.

HAPPY MEAL SONIA: No I don't! I ain't mental!!

TAINA: I know. But you're sick, Ma.

HAPPY MEAL SONIA: But if I'm sick, you're sick. We're the same, baby, you know that.

TAINA: No we're not, Ma. I love you but we're not the same.

(Sonia slaps Taina.)

HAPPY MEAL SONIA: We're the same, Taina! We're the same! You're blood from my blood, my heart, my soul—who took care of you? All these years?!

TAINA: I don't know, Ma—what years you talking about? When you were incarcerated? Those years? When you would chain me to the radiator when I was eight so you could go out—sucking dick, stealing wallets, blacking out—forgetting to come home?

HAPPY MEAL SONIA: That never happened!

TAINA: It did, but I ain't mad, I know you did your best—

HAPPY MEAL SONIA: That's right and let's not fight—let's go play cards.

TAINA: No. You gotta go. I'll come visit you.

HAPPY MEAL SONIA: No you won't.

TAINA: Of course I will. Ma: You think I like this? You think I wanna be not with you?

HAPPY MEAL SONIA: So come with me!

TAINA: I can't, Ma.

HAPPY MEAL SONIA: Then let me stay here!

TAINA: No. You sick. And I—I gotta have a life. Right, Ma? You had yours. I gotta have mine.

HAPPY MEAL SONIA: But I'll die in the hospital! I'll never get out! I'll die! Do you want that?

TAINA: I don't want you to die—

HAPPY MEAL SONIA: Well that's where you putting me. Putting me to die. And you know it.

TAINA: Not if you do what they say—

HAPPY MEAL SONIA: Taina. Baby. I ain't never gonna do what they say. When did I ever do what they said? No way. Look at me: I ain't never—gonna let them take my me—from me. Because I may be a lot of things—but I'm me. Me. Do you understand?

TAINA: I do, Ma. You're you. And I love you so much. But what about me, Ma? Don't you love me? What about me?

HAPPY MEAL SONIA: . . . Take me down to the Access-A-Ride. I don't wanna be with you no more.

TAINA: Ma—I wanna talk this out with you. They said I coulda just let them take you when you was asleep—that since you ain't lucid half the time, you'd wake up in a hospital and not know how you got there and that I should do it like that cuz it's more easy and less painful—but I said nah, my ma ain't retarded, my ma ain't a devil—I don't have to hide or run away, we could talk to each other. Right? We can still talk to each other, right? Right? Mami—right?

HAPPY MEAL SONIA: I wish you had done what they said. Let them take me at night. Like that, I wouldn't have known you left me, broke my heart, took their side, let me die.

TAINA: You're not gonna die, Ma!

HAPPY MEAL SONIA: When I hang myself, you gonna feel it when my neck snaps. Cracketa! You gonna hear that sound forever.

(Sonia spits in Taina's face.)

¡Puta Desgraciada Basura Asesina Pa Fuera I don't know you!

(Sonia takes her suitcase, exits and does not look back. Taina is alone. Weeps. After a moment, Jennifer enters.)

JENNIFER: Taina?

TAINA: Leave me alone, miss.

JENNIFER: You know I can't do that. Let me take you downstairs to the reading. Okay? And after, Mister Mobo, he finally got his work visa extended. There's gonna be cake.

(A beat. Then Jennifer takes Taina's hand, walks her downstairs. They enter the community room. In darkness, the women, except Sarge, are gathered. With a flashlight, Betty continues reading to them:)

BETTY WOODS: The men—they tasted me like I was golden honey, their mouths moving all over my body, switching places so that they could get a taste from between my legs.

MUNCHIES: Oh shit!

QUEEN SUGAR: Shut up! Go on, Betty—

BETTY WOODS: Ernesto bared his teeth against my nipples, flicking his green-eyed gaze up to me briefly as he did so, and the ecstasy was so intense I lost consciousness. Meanwhile, Diego did his job down below, savoring every taste and rendering me nearly frozen with pleasure. I gasped when the first orgasm moved through me, and, Ronaldo, between my legs, held me tight and close, sinking his fingers into my thighs and keeping me down to Earth. Alejandro was the first to move inside of me; I craved it, begged him for it, and he slid beneath me and pushed himself up to fill me in one swift motion. Marco was behind me, his hands on my hips, guiding me up and down, side to side. I was helpless to the lot of them, and yet, I knew I was the one calling all the shots—

(The women snap in unison.)

Should I go on?

VENUS RAMIREZ: Go girl!

ROCKAWAY ROSIE: Oh yes! Don't stop! Oh no no no no no!

BETTY WOODS: I tipped my head back and Thor brushed his lips over my throat. Pressing my hands to Umberto's strong chest for leverage, I moved harder, a little faster, finding a beat that seemed to suit all of us. I took ten men that night— and in the morning, fed them to the pigs. Such is the life of a queen being serviced—by her minions. The end.

(The women snap in unison. Jennifer is holding a cake and a carving knife.)

JENNIFER: Ladies! Please stay for cake to celebrate Mister Mobo's visa extension. Mobo, come in!

(Mobo enters with Mateo. The women clap. Munchies rises.)

MUNCHIES: Ah hell no! This fuckin' illegal, Wonder Bread Refugee Nigga—someone need to call Donald Trump on your ass!!

(She exits. Sarge wanders in somberly.)

JENNIFER: Mateo, help me with the cake.
MR. MOBO: Sarge, yes! Let's have some cake. Thank you, everybody.

(Rosie starts singing, the others slowly join in, as Mateo distributes cake—)

ROCKAWAY ROSIE: For he's a jolly good fellow, for he's a jolly good fellow, for he's a jolly good fell-el-oh—

(Suddenly, Rivera enters. She is stoic.)

MISS RIVERA: Quiet! Quiet!

(The room falls silent.)

Uh . . . Ladies. I just got a call. They found a body this morning by the Rotunda. In a dumpster. She had ID on her. It was Annabella O'Heaney.

(Beat.)

QUEEN SUGAR: Annabella who?
SARGE: . . . Bella!
LITTLE MELBA DIAZ: Oh my God—Bella!

(Sarge starts to shake—Mobo folds her into his arms.)

MISS RIVERA: The police may have some questions. If they do, please provide any information you got. I'm sorry. Mobo, congrats on the extension.

(*Mobo turns to address Rivera—*)

MR. MOBO: Thank you. But really—

(*Sarge slips out of Mobo's arms, runs to the cake, grabs the knife, and rushes Venus—*)

SARGE: You killed her! It was you! You!

(*Sarge goes to stab Venus. Venus raises her arm, takes the blow there, wrestles Sarge to the ground.*
The women circle them, trying to break it up. Finally, Mobo pulls them up off the ground. Sarge has the knife in her gut.)

ROCKAWAY ROSIE: Oh my God! Sarge! Sarge! (*To Venus*) You stabbed her! She's bleeding!
VENUS RAMIREZ: It was self-defense! You saw it! You saw it! Oh my God, call an ambulance.

(*Mobo carries Sarge in his arms, rushes out of the room.*
Blackout.)

SCENE 6

Miss Rivera's Office. Two Days Later.

Rivera is on the phone. Venus is sitting by her side.

MISS RIVERA: Miss Soto? Miss Soto, we need to try and place
Venus Ramirez in that LGBTQ shelter in Queens, she can
stay until we place her, I'm with her right now. And call
that VA in Ridgewood, when Sarge gets out of the hospital,
she's gotta go too. And call my daughter. Tell her, it's okay,
she can stay with her father until Monday, then she gets on
that plane and comes home. Plane, Miss Soto, plane—not
train! Thank you.

(Rivera hangs up.)

You'll be happier in Astoria. I wish you luck.

VENUS RAMIREZ: Thank you, miss.

MISS RIVERA: Clean up your act.

(Venus exits. Rivera takes a bottle out of her desk drawer. Pours a drink. Downs it . . . Picks up the phone to dial, when, a knock on the door—)

. . . Come in!

(Detective Sullivan enters first and authoritatively—Amy Golden is right on his tail, only slightly behind.)

DETECTIVE SULLIVAN: Grace Jenkins?

MISS RIVERA: . . . "Grace Jenkins"?

AMY GOLDEN *(To Sullivan: fast and quiet)*: That's not Grace Jenkins.

DETECTIVE SULLIVAN: You're not Grace Jenkins?

MISS RIVERA: Grace was my mentor. She's deceased. Who are you?

AMY GOLDEN: Um, if I may—I knew Mrs. Jenkins. Not well. But she was an incredible woman. And she didn't suffer fools.

MISS RIVERA: No she didn't.

AMY GOLDEN: I remember the funeral—Riverside Church—line around the block—

(Amy Golden extends her hand to Rivera, who shakes it, as—)

I'm Chief of Staff Amy Golden—from Councilman Neil Levine's office. This is Detective Sullivan, 24th Precinct—

MISS RIVERA: Bianca Rivera.

AMY GOLDEN: Oh I know. I'm a fan. *(To Sullivan)* Bianca's a two-time recipient of the Council's Special Citation for Excellence in Meritorious Service. *(To Rivera)* Grace Jenkins would be proud.

MISS RIVERA: How can I help you?

AMY GOLDEN: Well, Councilman Levine co-chairs the finance committee, and they're meeting with the mayor today—

MISS RIVERA: Oh yes—"Mayor de-Blah-Blah-Blah"! Promises Section 8 Housing, gives us poorly run privatized shelters instead. Tell Neil we need money here—

AMY GOLDEN: Absolutely—and I think you'll be very pleased with the councilman's proposed budget for the coming fiscal year, however, he did send me here today, in his stead, to help see you through the, uh, situation—

MISS RIVERA: What situation?

DETECTIVE SULLIVAN: We need you to relinquish your keys. I need to secure the building. Your clients and staff are outside, we need you to join them. Be available for questions.

MISS RIVERA: About what? Why do you need my keys?

AMY GOLDEN: It's going to be okay, Bianca—

DETECTIVE SULLIVAN *(To Amy Golden)*: Excuse me . . . *(To Rivera)* Where is the deceased, ma'am? Still on-site?

MISS RIVERA: The deceased? What are you talking about? Nobody died here. We had a client go missing two weeks ago, not that you people care—we reported it, never heard a word back.

DETECTIVE SULLIVAN: Gimme a name, I'll look into it. But my understanding concerning the matter at hand? Call logs show a 911 call placed from this location on the night of the victim's disappearance—approximately four A.M. last Wednesday.

MISS RIVERA: Four A.M.? . . .

DETECTIVE SULLIVAN: Traffic cameras picked up the victim's abduction, closed-circuit TV monitors place victim and suspect entering these premises—

MISS RIVERA: . . . Last Wednesday?

AMY GOLDEN: Bianca, any help you can give Detective Sullivan will only help your cause here——

DETECTIVE SULLIVAN *(To Amy Golden)*: Excuse me . . . *(To Rivera)* . . . Ms. Rivera?

MISS RIVERA: Four A.M. last Wednesday? . . . No. No, there isn't any deceased. I did get a call around that time, a staff member called me, Mister Mobo, but he said one of the clients had become hysterical saying, I don't know, her goat was missing—

AMY GOLDEN: The goat, yes!—

DETECTIVE SULLIVAN: Tell us about the goat. And this Mobo—he's the black fella?

MISS RIVERA: Yeah. But that woman was crazy, and—wait—hold up—you're here for a goat?

AMY GOLDEN: He is. We are.

MISS RIVERA: A goat? . . . You kidding me?! A goat?!

DETECTIVE SULLIVAN: Mister Skittles. Yes.

MISS RIVERA: What?

DETECTIVE SULLIVAN: Says here his name is Mister Skittles. The goat.

MISS RIVERA: The fuck you talkin' about?! You're really here for a goat?! A goat?! You locking down my building for what?! A goat??!!

AMY GOLDEN *(To Sullivan)*: May I? . . . Bianca: I know this is crazy, but this Skittles—he wasn't just some South Bronx Slaughterhouse Goat—he was one of those special goats sent to eat the weeds, the bad ivy—Special Upstate Goats—you know the ones—they have their own website, merchandising—they were on NY1, Eyewitness News—and Mister Skittles—he's what they call a pygmy, he's little, very cute, so kids adore him. Adults too. And you know how people get about animals—

DETECTIVE SULLIVAN: We got like five of your neighbors here reporting seeing the goat entering this location that night. Now, I don't necessarily believe any of them—everybody know you people are not well liked here. That said, we've obtained a credible tip that one of your residents murdered the goat.

MISS RIVERA: "Murdered"?!

AMY GOLDEN: I know, I agree—but killing cute animals, I mean, you know how Upper West Siders can be—

DETECTIVE SULLIVAN: Bottom line, it's a public safety issue.

MISS RIVERA: Ya know: A year ago, an actual human being was raped and murdered on these premises—we could barely get the cops to take a report!

DETECTIVE SULLIVAN: I'm just doing my job. Give me your keys, ma'am—

MISS RIVERA: I need to speak to the councilman! Or your captain! All these uppity neighbors with their strollers and "let's go buy a ten-dollar cupcake"—they don't want us here, you know that, I know that! But see—I got actual human residents here with actual human needs—women, young girls who have been beaten, raped, abused, homeless, neglected, disposable, many of them no different than me—or your wife, Detective—or you, Amy Golden—and now you gonna try an' come up here in my office, take my keys, talking to me about some goddamn—some stupid fucking goat?! Well no—fuck that! And fuck that goat! My ladies need me and they need to be here—

(Rivera rises and advances toward Sullivan. Suddenly, Joey enters.)

JOEY FRESCO: Miss Rivera, hold up—

DETECTIVE SULLIVAN: Who are you?

JOEY FRESCO: Joey Fresco. Custodial services. I just. I left something in my locker, I had to get it. But then I overheard y'all—and you Miss Rivera—and you know, about the goat and all, and none of this ain't Miss Rivera's fault. And I don't even like her. And I'm pretty sure she don't like me—

AMY GOLDEN: Do you have information for us?

JOEY FRESCO: I know where the goat is.

AMY GOLDEN: Where? Tell us.

JOEY FRESCO: Okay, I don't know nuthin about nuthin about how this goat came to be—you know—fuckin' dead, but, you know, however, I did come to, I guess, discover the body of you know, the goat, and, well—

DETECTIVE SULLIVAN: Where is he now?

JOEY FRESCO: Well, I wrapped him in a sheet, then put him and the sheet into, like, an industrial-strength garbage bag—you know, the black ones?—and then I took the Number 5 bus with him, the bus stop is right over there on the corner—

DETECTIVE SULLIVAN: You took a dead goat on the Number 5 bus?

JOEY FRESCO: I did. And then the crosstown bus on 125th, I mean, I live by there, I was going home anyway—

AMY GOLDEN: Where's the goat, Mister Fresco?

JOEY FRESCO: Buried. By the East River. I was gonna toss him. But I thought burial was like more I don't know, and, I'm superstitious an' shit, so better to not take chances, you know? But Miss Rivera here, she didn't know nuthin about it. About the disposing of the body an' shit. We kept it from her. I mean I did. But she didn't know. Am I gonna be arrested?

DETECTIVE SULLIVAN: Just take me to the location.

(As Sullivan leads Joey out—)

JOEY FRESCO: I'm sorry, Miss Rivera. I was just trying to protect our place, ya know?

MISS RIVERA: I know.

JOEY FRESCO: If they lock me up—tell Venus wait for me.

(They exit. Rivera takes out bottle, pours herself a drink.)

MISS RIVERA: So—what's gonna happen now?

AMY GOLDEN: Call our office in the morning. Neil will advise
you. I know that our constituents and REBNY, those real-
estate whores, they've been trying to close the doors on
this place since the day you first opened.

MISS RIVERA: And now they get their wish. Thanks to you.

AMY GOLDEN: Bianca—I intend to fight for you, and for this
place—

MISS RIVERA: You wanna leave here with teeth, stop acting like
you give a shit.

*(Rivera jots down some names on a piece of paper, hands it to
Amy Golden.)*

Here.

AMY GOLDEN: What's this?

MISS RIVERA: I got two minors in residence and a young girl in
her early twenties. One is a straight-A student, the other
has turned his life around, and the girl in her twenties
badly needs—deserves—something—anything—good to
happen for her. Get them placed somewhere safe.

AMY GOLDEN: I'll make sure Neil gets this—

MISS RIVERA: I wouldn't trust Neil Levine to pass the salt. No.
You do it. Get it done. Like you got this done today.

AMY GOLDEN: For the record, I'm not into women tearing other
women down.

MISS RIVERA: You gonna help my kids or what?

AMY GOLDEN: . . . You should think about not drinking.

MISS RIVERA: Excuse me?

AMY GOLDEN: My boss was terrified of Grace Jenkins. This
never would've happened on her watch.

MISS RIVERA: You saying this is my fault??!! I work sixteen hours
a day, six days a week, understaffed, underfunded, under-
fucking— Hey, where you going?!

(Amy Golden puts her card on Rivera's table.)

AMY GOLDEN: My cell phone is on the back there. If you ever wanna go to a meeting.

MISS RIVERA: Meeting? What about my kids? Hey! Hey!

(Amy Golden exits.)

SCENE 7

Exodus. Day.

Inside, the building is being broken down to be evacuated.

Joey, Mobo and Jennifer are stacking chairs, breaking down beds, and periodically exiting through the alley to place large black garbage bags of refuse on the edge of the sidewalk for trash pickup.

Rosie sits on the stoop with her suitcase. On one side of her is Mateo and on the other side is Melba.

LITTLE MELBA DIAZ: Mateo's depressed, Miss Rosie.

MATEO: I ain't depressed.

LITTLE MELBA DIAZ: He going to foster care and his moms going to hospice in the Bronx.

MATEO: It ain't a hospice—it's a hospital.

LITTLE MELBA DIAZ: It's a hospice, Miss Rosie.

MATEO: It's called Calvary HOSPITAL. A hospital is a hospital.

LITTLE MELBA DIAZ: A hospital may be a hospital, but Calvary be a hospice: Patients check in but they don't check out.

ROCKAWAY ROSIE: Oh, Melba—no no no no Melba, go fetch Wanda, okay? She—she knows how to talk to Mateo.

LITTLE MELBA DIAZ: Okay, Miss Rosie.

(Melba exits inside. Rosie can see Mateo is very upset, but she doesn't know what to say. She goes into her purse, pulls out some peppermints.)

ROCKAWAY ROSIE: Mateo—want a mint?

MATEO: Nah.

ROCKAWAY ROSIE: Have a mint. It's, it's, you know—when I was a young girl and something bad would happen in my house, I'd run downstairs and, and—sit by my landlady's kitchen window, because I knew she would see me there, and then she would come out, and she knew there was trouble upstairs in my house, so, she would give me a mint—a red mint, or a green mint—my landlady, she was deaf, so she couldn't hear when there was trouble, but then when she would see me, always she gave me a mint—and it was—soothing. Very soothing. So have a mint.

MATEO: Miss Rosie: Father Miguel's going back to Jersey, plus they taking my moms away, plus they trying to place me in Brownsville, plus Miss Wanda gonna die soon, plus Little Melba prolly gonna be turning tricks again, plus I ain't never gonna see Taina no more—

ROCKAWAY ROSIE: Oh—you're fond of Taina?

MATEO: She okay. You know what I'm "fond" of, Rosie? I'm fond of here. I wanna stay here.

ROCKAWAY ROSIE: Oh Mateo, I know.

(Rosie wraps her arm around him—he lets her.)

Okay. Okay—now have a damn mint! Have it!

(He accepts a mint, unwraps it, pops it his mouth.)

Okay, now—Wanda will be here soon, she's good with the talking.

MATEO: She don't eat, she trying to die—fuck Miss Wanda.

ROCKAWAY ROSIE: Hey! Hey hey hey! You wanna smack? . . . Now, Wanda, she's good with words, not me. Wait for Wanda. But Mateo—you're a good boy. A family boy. And life? It's not always fair, okay? Oh! Like—the movie!— yes!—the movie!

MATEO: What movie?

ROCKAWAY ROSIE: That you like! With, you know, oh—in real life he's bad behavior, but, but in the movies? He makes good movies, usually, the actor, oh you know, you know!

MATEO: Kevin Hart?

ROCKAWAY ROSIE: No! Oh Jesus Mary and Joseph—the movie! The movie! WE watched it—you, me, that girl, the poor girl who died?

MATEO: Keisha?

ROCKAWAY ROSIE: Keisha, yes!

MATEO: *Gladiator?*

ROCKAWAY ROSIE: Yes! *Gladiator! Gladiator!* Now, that man, the Gladiator—

MATEO: Russell Crowe.

ROCKAWAY ROSIE: Yes. In the movie, he's a slave. Everything's bad, his wife, everything, he's all alone, tragedy, treachery, doom!—and, you know—it's all NOT FAIR. But Mateo, the Gladiator, he kept going, right? He didn't give up! And, and—what happened at the end of the movie?

MATEO: . . . He died.

ROCKAWAY ROSIE: What?! He didn't die!

MATEO: He died, Miss Rosie.

ROCKAWAY ROSIE: HE DID NOT—Oh . . . Oh, yes. Yes, he did. Oh no. He died. I'm a jackass. Words—I'm just no good.

MATEO: Nah, Miss Rosie—he died, but, he didn't never give up. That's what you was sayin', right? Life ain't fair but don't give up.

ROCKAWAY ROSIE: Yes!! Yes!! But no! No. Because life isn't like that. Most people give up. Life is too big. So don't feel bad if you give up. Oh oh—I'm sorry for my tears, and you shouldn't ever give up, don't listen to me! Oh oh oh good—look, there's Wanda coming.

(Rosie rises, takes her little suitcase.)

MATEO: Miss Rosie, gimme your bag. I'll walk you to the bus.

ROCKAWAY ROSIE: Oh, no no no. Wanda's coming. Wanda. Wanda's good.

(Mateo takes Rosie's bag.)

MATEO: You good too, miss. C'mon.

(They walk down the block. Melba enters with Wanda, wheels her to her spot. Sugar and Munchies exit the front door. Munchies has her stuff in a plastic garbage bag over her shoulder.)

MUNCHIES: Okay, bitches. If y'all see Sarge, tell her I'm a be at my aunt's house in Coney Island.

QUEEN SUGAR: I don't think no one gonna ever see Sarge again.

WANDA WHEELS: I think you right on that.

(Melba takes a paper out of her pocket—)

LITTLE MELBA DIAZ: Hold up! Munchies, this for you. *(Reads)* "Beautiful eyes, young but wise. Funny as shit but fierce and legit. Good mother to her seed, True Black Queen indeed. Crunchy Munchie who lent me her scrunchie—

already told her I missed her, fuck Mobo who dissed her, I hope his penis get a blister and his ass gets a fister—but this ain't no time for no show-off tongue twister, thank you for your heart—cuz I ain't never had no big sister. Till now, it's true. Till you—true blue." Here. Keep it.

(Munchies is moved.)

MUNCHIES: Okay. But no hugs . . . Aaiight. Well, I ain't the good-bye type, so y'all be good, fam. Peace!

(Munchies exits. Taina pops her head out the building.)

TAINA: Melba. Miss Rivera got like mad stuff she say we can have if we go to her office now.
LITTLE MELBA DIAZ: Bet!

(Melba exits with Taina. Wanda and Sugar are alone.)

WANDA WHEELS: Your name gonna be on my life insurance whether you help me or not. So the courteous thing for you to do would be to help me.
QUEEN SUGAR: Stop.
WANDA WHEELS: Cuz I'll just do it myself—but what if I live? I knew an actress once—dramatic—French—French equals dramatic—we were on tour, she swallowed a bottle of pills, drank a quart of vodka, cut her wrists and neck, tied a plastic bag over her head, hung a sign around her neck said, "Ne pas ressusciter," then set her dressing room on fire—
QUEEN SUGAR: Oh that's a lie! You a silver-tongued devil!
WANDA WHEELS: She lived. The woman lived. Brain damage, burned up, paralyzed, incapable of speech. She lived another nine years. I told myself right then and there, when I kill myself, I'm hiring help.

QUEEN SUGAR: Mm hmm. That's me? Hired help? You're selfish. You're so selfish. We leave when God say. And people, us out here in the world, we need you.

WANDA WHEELS: Do you need me so much you prefer me alive and in a cage? Until I was forty, I lived a life of freedom. I want my freedom back. I want it back. I've had enough. Enough. I trust you. I need you. Release me. Do you think I'm crazy?

QUEEN SUGAR: No.

WANDA WHEELS: Do you think I haven't thought this through?

QUEEN SUGAR: I know you have.

WANDA WHEELS: And do you believe me when I say we have good times, good conversations, I love you, I care about you, you make my life better—but even with all that—I am in pain, I am trapped, I am overwhelmed with anger and regret and shame and physical pain, and a deep, deep bottomless void of depression that suffocates me every day from the inside out and that maybe—just maybe—I know best and I deserve the right to choose my path? I know it's a lot. But I'm just asking you to help me. And to believe me when I say—thank you, thank you, thank you—but I have had enough . . .

(Beat. Their eyes lock. Sugar stares. Wanda allows herself to be seen. Lights fade.)

SCENE 8

Building Exterior. Late Afternoon.

Sarge sits on a milk crate. Her suitcase by her side. She looks like hell. After a beat, Rivera exits the building carrying a box with her personal items.

MISS RIVERA: Sarge.

SARGE: I just came back for my stuff. Now I'm just waiting on my peoples.

MISS RIVERA: Good.

SARGE: Yeah. Staying at my niece's in Jersey. Got a backyard.

MISS RIVERA: Nice.

SARGE: A swimming pool too. And air hockey.

MISS RIVERA: Okay. Your wound healing up?

SARGE: Yep. Sorry if I caused trouble.

MISS RIVERA: . . . Okay then . . .

SARGE: Thanks for everything, miss. Everybody know you done your best.

MISS RIVERA: Um . . . Thanks.

(Rivera goes to exit.)

SARGE: . . . You need help with them boxes?

MISS RIVERA: I'm okay.

SARGE: I could carry 'em for you. To like the subway or whatever.

MISS RIVERA: I'm good . . . Stay well, Sarge.

SARGE: I'm trying, miss. Still—ain't no way to treat a veteran though, right? Not you. Not you, miss. I mean, people. I served my country, right?

MISS RIVERA: Yes you did.

SARGE: I ain't saying I'm special . . .

MISS RIVERA: I know what you're saying.

SARGE: Yeah . . . Ain't seen my kid in five years, ya know?

MISS RIVERA: I'm sorry.

SARGE: Thinks I'm crazy. Violent. My own daughter. You believe that shit?

MISS RIVERA: Do you have her number? I could call her.

SARGE: Nah . . . I mean, Only the Strong Survive, right, miss?

MISS RIVERA: You're a survivor, Sarge.

SARGE: Yeah. I survived.

(Beat.)

MISS RIVERA: Okay then.

SARGE: Okay.

(Rivera starts to go, then—)

Miss Rivera?

MISS RIVERA: Yes?

SARGE: . . . Take me with you?

MISS RIVERA: . . . Sarge—

SARGE: Take me with you. I ain't got nobody. And I think I'm not okay. I'm not okay, am I? Right? Right? Right I'm not okay?

MISS RIVERA: I could take you to the VA.

SARGE: What's the VA gonna do? I ain't right. I ain't okay. And I'm way past the fuckin' VA.

MISS RIVERA: I can't take you with me, Sarge. But I could—

SARGE: Just tell me I'm not okay—cuz I'm not okay, right? Just tell me the truth. I'm not okay, right?

MISS RIVERA: . . . You're not.

SARGE: And I prolly won't never be, right?

MISS RIVERA: Maybe not.

SARGE: And I need help, right? Like a lot of help, right?

MISS RIVERA: Right.

SARGE: And people are afraid of me?

MISS RIVERA: Yes.

SARGE: A danger to myself and others, like how they say?

MISS RIVERA: You are, yes.

SARGE: And who gives a fuck about me? Nobody, right?

MISS RIVERA: Sarge—

SARGE: Please, Miss Rivera. Just tell me the truth. I got no place to go and nobody gives a fuck about me, right?

MISS RIVERA: I wish I could help. I tried to have this conversation with you—how many times?

SARGE: I know, I wouldn't listen.

MISS RIVERA: No.

SARGE: I know. I remember. And you can't help me no more, right?

MISS RIVERA: Sarge—

SARGE: Right? Just tell me. Cuz my head's just about split in two and bleeding from both sides.

MISS RIVERA: . . . Okay . . . Nobody gives a fuck, Sarge. Not really. And I can't help you no more. I can't. Not no more.

SARGE: Yeah. Yeah, okay. Thank you. Thank you, Miss Rivera. Thank you.

(Rivera heads up the block. Sarge is alone. Sarge fishes through her suitcase, pulls out an old piece of toast wrapped in foil, starts eating it. Time passes.
 A couple walks by—)

Spare some change?

END OF PLAY

Theatre Communications Group would like to offer our special thanks to Betsy Pitts for her generous support of the publication of Halfway Bitches Go Straight to Heaven *by Stephen Adly Guirgis*

———

BETSY PITTS serves as the Secretary of the Board of Atlantic Theater Company and is a member of TCG's National Council for the American Theatre.

TCG books sponsored by Betsy Pitts include:

Halfway Bitches Go Straight to Heaven by Stephen Adly Guirgis
The Ground on Which I Stand: 25th Anniversary Edition by August Wilson

THEATRE COMMUNICATIONS GROUP's mission is to lead for a just and thriving theatre ecology. Through its Core Values of Activism, Artistry, Diversity, and Global Citizenship, TCG advances a better world for theatre and a better world because of theatre. TCG Books is the largest independent trade publisher of dramatic literature in North America, with 19 Pulitzer Prizes for Drama on its book list. The book program commits to the lifelong career of its playwrights, keeping all of their plays in print. TCG Books' authors include: Annie Baker, Nilo Cruz, Jackie Sibblies Drury, Larissa FastHorse, Athol Fugard, Aleshea Harris, Jeremy O. Harris, Quiara Alegría Hudes, David Henry Hwang, Michael R. Jackson, Branden Jacobs-Jenkins, Adrienne Kennedy, The Kilroys, Tony Kushner, Young Jean Lee, Tracy Letts, Martyna Majok, Dominique Morisseau, Lynn Nottage, Dael Orlandersmith, Suzan-Lori Parks, Sarah Ruhl, Stephen Sondheim, Paula Vogel, Anne Washburn, and August Wilson, among many others.

Support TCG's work in the theatre field by becoming a member or donor: www.tcg.org

tcg